The Corporate Hustle!

The Guide to Winning in Corporate America.

Cornelius Z. Jones

The Corporate Hustle

The Guide to Winning in Corporate America.

R.O.A.R. Publishing Group
581 N. Park Ave. Ste. #725
Apopka, FL 32704
321-312-0744
www.RoarPublishingGroup.com

Published in the United States of America
ISBN: 978-1-948936-31-6
$16.95

Table of Contents

INTRODUCTION

As we meander through the corporate world of living, we will find that we are all meant to accomplish something great. Although most often we coast through living our lives, we may find ourselves not living our best life, even if we pretend as if we are. Well, *"The Corporate Hustle"* is no different; we go from job to job or promotion to promotion only to feel incomplete once we get to the next level. Why is that the case? Well, this is the reason for this book...I am going to share the secrets on how we can find our passion in Corporate America, as well as outside of the workplace.

When we attempt to pursue our lives through the mirror of the corporates, we may sometimes feel intimidated by the ability to meet or exceed the expectations set for us. As a result, we find ourselves coasting our way through our role on a wing and a prayer. I am not saying that a wing and a prayer is a bad thing; however, after reading this book, we are going to put an end to it. I am going to share the information needed to get whoever's willing to the top of their game, and the information needed to keep them there.

I have been in the corporate game a few decades now. The compiled information that I have today from my "Corporate Hustle," I didn't have a clue about when I first started, nor was it given when I entered Corporate America. If I had this information I am about to share, who knows how far up the corporate ladder I would have climbed. Nevertheless, it is my reasonable service to prepare others with the information, secrets, and know-how on creating a win-win situation out of every aspect of life. In this book, here is what I am going to do for you:

- I am going to give you the secrets to making people like you.
- I am going to prepare you with the information to keep you from making costly mistakes in the corporate world.
- I am going to give you the secrets on how to avoid becoming tongue-tied.
- I am going to give you advice on how to save money and become a millionaire.
- I am going to share with you how to run a business or build your own business.
- I am going to share the secrets on how to increase your overall revenue.
- I am going to share how to maximize your salary to build your own empire.
- I am going to share the secrets on how to release your creative giant from within.
- I am going to teach you how to mind map your life.

- I am going to share the secrets on how to leave a legacy.

The Corporate Hustle" has been designed to assist in the developmental secrets of success. I am a true rags to riches phenomena, and so are you. If you follow my lead in this book, you will succeed, guaranteed.

"*The Corporate Hustle*" is real. The power behind the hustle is the legacy we leave behind. If we have nothing to show for the hustle that we have to go through on a daily basis, then it is time to rethink, revamp, or reappropriate a few things. I am not saying what we are doing is wrong, all I am saying is that we are the mentors for tomorrow's up and coming leaders; and, we need to pinpoint what we are doing and the reasons why. On this note, it is my reasonable service to provide the information, concepts, and principles needed to help assist in becoming a mentor or mentee.

It is not a coincidence that "*The Corporate Hustle*" has made it into your hands. This book is encapsulated with profound information that will revolutionize your life, as you begin to bring forth a new corporate mindset. If you have not noticed by now, your lifestyle and business go hand in hand. We depend on companies to cater to our lifestyles, and we depend upon working for a company to finance it. Therefore, in our capitalization process, it is imperative that we find what works for us, as well as being able to own our truth to make the corporate monotony work for us and not against us.

Regardless of whether we are an employee, business owner, contractor, or homemaker, our jobs are crucial in order to make our realities work. We all have some sort of influence on something or someone; therefore, we cannot downplay or upplay our position in life. We are all given an equal right to succeed no matter what, with whatever our heart desires, and with whomever. So, there is no need to have the crab in the bucket mentality. We must wish everyone well because what God has for us, it will be, period!

In the hustle of life, I've had several people ask, "Why am I being overlooked for promotions?" "Why am I not getting a fair raise?" "Why doesn't my boss favor me?" "Why do my coworkers avoid me?" My response has always been, "How is your attitude?" "Are you friendly?" "Are you approachable?" "Do you greet your coworkers?" "How is your character?" By asking those questions, it gets their wheels to turning to see what their coworkers are doing that they are not.

In corporate America, we must establish our worthiness. If we are not perceived as being valuable to a company, more than likely, we may get overlooked. Is it fair? Absolutely not, if we are qualified. But here again, if our worthiness has not been proven, then those who are making the decisions may not feel comfortable with our lack of tenacity. Nonetheless, all is not lost. I have the information in the pages of this book that is going to change how you think, change your method of operation, and reveal the secrets on how to make all things work together for your good.

CHAPTER 1

THE CORPORATE MINDSET

"The Corporate Hustle" is all about the developmental phase of our upcoming ventures. What we are going to do is take the acquired knowledge, skills, and know-how and build progressive empires for ourselves and others. The alliances that we have assimilated and will attain is of the utmost importance in creating good quality people skills in our personal and professional life. When we are positively connected, it provides the freedom and the flexibility needed to soar beyond our wildest dreams.

As we begin the developmental process, the corporate mindset starts with us taking good care of ourselves, especially the mind. When we feel good, we produce better results for those who have taken a risk on our talent. Now if we think good thoughts, that is like icing on the cake, and there is no limit on what we can achieve or do for others.

When developing the corporate mindset, it is imperative that we dig deep. Dig deep? Yes, we must dig deep within ourselves to understand who we are as an individual, as well as why we are here. Without this formal understanding of self, it leaves room to try to fit in, to become brainwashed, or to become bullied. The ultimate goal here is to hone in on the value of respect. In my opinion, the only way to master the element of connection is to value the respect of ourselves, while respecting the differences of others. How does this compare with knowing self and respecting self? In order to truly understand ourselves, respect must be intact; if not, there will be an inner struggle from within that seeps over into our personal and professional relationships.

Of course, we try to keep our personal and professional relationships separate, but it is only a matter of time before they collide. Therefore, we must always become a representative of the corporate mindset; it is not good to risk our livelihood for a fleeting moment. From the 1990s, there is a phrase saying, "What would Jesus do?" which, in my opinion, is a relevant question to ask oneself; however, more importantly, we must become ever so cognizant about "What would Corporate do?" With this wave of social media, we cannot become reckless about our corporate image…keep in mind, every time we walk out the door, we represent something or someone.

The corporate image has become a little lax, but it is essential to polish up our image. We do not have to make a fashion statement, but it is imperative to make sure that we are well-groomed. We do not have to spend a lot of money or wear designer labels in order to do so. Here are a few things that will assist:

1. Take care of your health.
2. Eat healthily.
3. Drink water.
4. Exercise to keep oxygen flowing to your brain.
5. Develop your confidence.
6. Keep a smile on your face as much as possible.
7. Wear a hairstyle that fits your personality.
8. Take care of your skin.
9. If you wear makeup, keep it natural looking.
10. Keep a nice wardrobe with shoes that compliment your outfit.
11. Do not wear clothes that are too tight, too revealing, or too short.

With the saying, "I do whatever I want" is not an ideal colloquialism for those who are aiming for the top. We must remember, in the corporate world, everything is not about us! There are people above and below us; we do not want our negative behaviors or our corporate image to affect those who are running in their own lane, trying to get to the top as well.

Once we can understand our negative energy, we are then able to release it, making it work on our behalf. The power of being able to let go of anger, fear, frustration, hatred, resentment, etc., gives us the ability to manage them accordingly while being able to mastermind our success. It also provides us with the ability to change them into something positive to create a positive lifestyle as we make *"The Corporate Hustle"* our empire building a legacy of greatness.

There are times in life where we are in the corporate world, but somehow in the midst of life happening, we seemed to have lost our hustle. The spontaneity that we once had appears as if it has gone into hiding. What is the problem? Our thoughts or self-talk could very well be the issue here. As technology is changing rapidly, we must do likewise…we cannot sit back and allow the newfound technology to zap our years of skills, talent, and know-how.

Being in the corporate world for over thirty years, I have witnessed many changes. Without a doubt, we cannot defy the old-school wisdom or the hustle and grind in the innate ability to get the job done. In order to maximize our business or professional skills, we must take a look at:

- Our performance.
- Our effectiveness.
- Our integrity.
- Our level of communication.

In *"The Corporate Hustle,"* we are looking for assets, opportunities, and targets. By knowing this, we are able to become highly effective in locking in on our goals or accomplishments. Our peak-performance is the desired goal, but we must have some sort of leverage. That means we need to focus on the product or service, the level of quality, the expenses, and how we are going to get the product sold. This is where our systems, strategies, and concepts come into play. Keep in mind, we are in this to win; therefore, we need to get this information on paper, mapping it out, creating a business plan, or developing a growth model will do the trick. If you are the product, then so be it! The same rules apply. The goal is GROWTH, period.

If we are managing or growing a business, here are a few things that are needed:

1. A company newsletter.
2. A referral system.
3. Continuous learning with seminars and workshops.
4. Interactive website.
5. Marketing.
6. Offer special promotions or contests.
7. Sponsor charity events.
8. Strategic Alliances.
9. The ability to cross-sell products.
10. Trade show participation.
11. Offer guarantees or risk-free purchases.

In *"The Corporate Hustle,"* when prospecting:

1. We need to get the attention of our prospects.
2. We need to spark their interest by getting them connected to our product mentally or emotionally.
3. We need to spark the desire to know and want more.
4. We need to close the sale with a call to action.

Our breakthrough strategies are in the palm of our hand. All we need to do is learn how to market it, create innovation for it, and do great business with outright integrity. Regardless of whether we are working for someone or whether we are working for ourselves, we are our best brand. If we do not know this or if we do not own this one fact, we lose our credibility instantly! Therefore, when we present what we have to offer, there cannot be any residing doubt because it could contaminate our brand.

CHAPTER 2

THE CORPORATE PRINCIPLES

Our corporate beliefs may or may not align with our true expectations; however, we must learn how to fit into the vision the company has set forth. If not, we will have too many visions running an organization, which leads to chaos or confusion above and below the surface.

"*The Corporate Hustle*" is about creating the platform of positive values that will increase our bottom line in whatever our occupation of choice happens to be. Our life philosophies play a vital role in doing business because this is where all of our talents, attitudes, habits, hang-ups, successes, and failures collide. If we are not ready to understand and deal with the differences in others, we are in for a rude awakening. In my opinion, we always want to be the answer to the problem, not the cause of them! Therefore, it is imperative that we gear up with our positive people skills and tools that go beyond the expectations set for us.

My goal is to become a mentor that opens unlimited opportunities and possibilities for everyone who has a desire to go to the next level. There have been times when I have made a few mistakes or regretted making a few unwise decisions, but it made me a stronger businessman and entrepreneur.

When faced with challenges, I have learned to develop them into learning opportunities. As a matter of fact, it is my mishaps in life that inspired me to write this book with such precision, tenacity, and love. Sometimes, it is when the odds are stacked against us or when our back is up against the wall, we push beyond our self-imposed limitations.

Although we have personal obligations, it does not exempt us from becoming a team player with our ability to become proactive. Thinking about or taking care of a need before it is presented has a viable impact on our effectiveness. This principle can indeed bring our talents or skills to the forefront if we master it. The underlying principles of business will work for those who are in or out of the corporate world as long as they are effectively applying them.

On my journey up the ladder of success, I learned the value of helping others along the way. There were some who did not want or need my help, but it was my responsibility to do my part in providing them the opportunity to have the necessary information required to go to the next level. What I have found is that I am just as responsible for sharing the information as I am for withholding it. We must give others the opportunity of having what we have to offer to keep our hands blessed with more information. In so many words, in order to get more knowledge or wisdom, we must be willing to share it with others with no strings attached. The moment we release the information, we free ourselves to receive more because we did not exhibit selfishness.

It is incredible how selfishness will cause us to miss out on steps, overlook steps, or break steps while we are climbing the ladder of success. When our greed or ego causes us to disrupt the relational connections with others, we will find that we will begin to create a hostile environment for those who are committed to the growth process of success.

I must say, home training goes hand-in-hand with corporate training and vice versa. We cannot have too many Chiefs and no Indians when building a business, building an empire, or leaving a legacy. The moment I speak of home training, most would cringe; but it is imperative that we create a balanced lifestyle between work and family. If not, the imbalance will become evident in every area of our lives with or without our permission.

In my opinion, it is an atrocity if we treat our coworkers better than our family or treat our family better than we treat our coworkers. We must find a way to treat everyone with love, kindness, and compassion to ensure we are creating positive energy. Even if people do not like us, we are obligated to do the right thing! We must become ever so careful about burning bridges with people because we never know when we need to cross that bridge again.

CHAPTER 3

MASTERMIND SUCCESS

The power of masterminding our success is all about being able to think inside, outside, around, and through the box. The best way that I have found to release our true mastery is to write them down. When we try to keep everything in our head, it will get entangled with the elements of everyday life! In my opinion, this is what we want to avoid in order to think on a different level. Once the thought, idea, plan, or inclination is written down, we are then able to revisit, rewrite, rethink, revamp, reanalyze, etc. This will indeed put the ball in our court, especially when we need a second opinion because people cannot see what's in our mind unless we create a paper trail for them to see what we are seeing.

Here is a secret, if someone cannot see what we see once it is written out, then we must redo it until the vision is seen crystal clear. Our power lies in the ability to paint pictures even if we proclaim not to be an artist! In my opinion, we are all creative, and if we can hone in on this element of our creativity, we will find our ability to create a niche in the corporate workplace that makes us hard to replace.

Personally, I have developed several niche areas in my "*Corporate Hustle.*" First and foremost, I am a Mechanical Engineer with a Master's Degree in Business and Marketing. I am also a qualified lubrication specialist in rotary equipment; and, a certified quality assurance and control advisor as it relates to overall project design, engineering, procurement, construction, start-ups, and completions. In addition, I am a successful entrepreneur with several businesses. Even with all of this, just so we are clear, we are all replaceable; therefore, we cannot allow our creativity to make us pompous.

Once we begin to listen to the voice from within regarding our ideas, thoughts, or defaults, we are then able to become proactive regarding our discoveries, solutions, or direction in life. When we are able to give of ourselves freely, we are better able to help others without any form of ulterior motives.

If for some reason we find ourselves a little gloomy, we can break that cycle by helping someone in need. Listen, we are so blessed, and there are times when the issues of life will blind us from seeing our blessings. But if we are able to reach beyond our self-imposed limitations and reach back to help someone without having a motive...it will shatter the blinders on our eyes giving us more of a reason to be grateful as opposed to being judgmental. Plus, most of the time, we are in a gloomy mood is due to the fact that we are internally judging ourselves, our situation, etc., which puts a boomerang in our element of gratefulness. However, it is our responsibility to reverse the role or the effects of our present state of mind; and, now we have the secret on how to do so.

The key to my success is to never stop learning! We must continue to grow, know, and learn more than we did the day before, especially in our field of interest. Plus, we cannot be afraid to expand our territory with great information as well. We are in a time where we have a smorgasbord of great information at our fingertips for FREE, why would we not take advantage of it? There are classes, internships, groups, and mentorship programs that can keep us on the leading edge of our field if we have a desire to increase in knowledge, wisdom, and stature. Here are a few things we need to know about a corporate business:

1. A company must have a vision.
2. A company must have a business plan.
3. A company should have good ethics.
4. A company should have a good plan of action.
5. A company needs a structured budget.
6. A company works best when marketing is involved.
7. A company works best when they have good, quality products and services.
8. A company works best when they treat their employees and vendors with love and respect.
9. A company works best when they exhibit excellent customer service.
10. A company works best when they continue to train their employees for the betterment of the company.
11. A company works best when they motivate and inspire their employees.

12. A company works best when employees are able to have fun occasionally.
13. A company works best when they listen to their employees.
14. A company works best when we separate our personal lives from our professional lives. There must be a balance between the two...bringing personal problems to work is a big no-no.
15. A company works best when they are able to give back to the community.

These tips are applicable if we are in the corporate arena, whether we own a business, or whether we are making plans to venture out into some sort of partnership. Keep in mind that we cannot limit ourselves...there are times when we are going to have to create opportunities for ourselves and others. So, don't get stuck in a rut if something is not working...find a way. Sometimes we may have to dig deep or get a little creative with our product or service. In my opinion, if we push hard enough, the door will open as long as we believe and keep a positive mental attitude.

Throughout my journey in the corporate arena, one principle that I have learned is to disengage in the need to complain. If it is necessary to make mention of something, I simply voice my concerns in a positive demeanor with a possible solution or a fact-finding question, and I leave it alone. My goal is to maximize my full potential without becoming paralyzed with menial complaints while exhibiting a whole lot of patience.

As progress occurs, it is vital to keep track of it. For me, a success map works quite well. But more importantly, it helps us to keep up with the small blessings or accomplishments. This gives us an opportunity to reflect back, to appreciate how far we have come. For the most part, it is always good to track our mistakes and failures along the way because it creates a trail of corporate wisdom that most people overlook. It also establishes a cornerstone of exceptional lessons that we are able to put into action or share.

In "*The Corporate Hustle*," it is best to always be ready to take notes at any given moment. We need to get random thoughts on paper; even when we are in a meeting, we need to take notes. As a matter of fact, start keeping a notepad by the bed; after reading this book, all sorts of ideas may spring up. Our notes may not mean much right now, but it is a possibility that those notes may play a vital role in our goal setting or mapping process. Better yet, we may need those notes when we are developing a system or strategy for a specific project. Who knows...just write it down and sort it out later.

CHAPTER 4

PLAYING TO WIN

In the hustle of life, there is a code of ethics in place to keep us in touch with reality. Once we step outside of them, we will find ourselves vulnerable to unnecessary negativity, chaos, and bad habits. Plus, when it comes down to living our best life, we do not want the elements of foolishness to lay claim to our empire, wealth, health, success, or opportunities.

As a partaker of *"The Corporate Hustle,"* self-control, self-discipline, self-analysis, and self-awareness are key players in the game of life. Being out of control is a game-changer for us, especially when it comes down to doing business. If we want the best of what life has to offer, it is imperative that we keep our cool, while setting a guard over our mouth and thoughts.

An expression is our power, or it can be our downfall; therefore, we must keep it on the positive side of the spectrum to make it work on our behalf. Listen, greatness is all around us, and it is within us. If we want our portion of the pie, then we have to step up to the plate to carve out our share. Who wants everyone to pass them by? Who wants their greatness to lay dormant? No one, right?

Now is the time to prepare the way for your greatness to come forth. You have been around the block long enough; it is time out with the rat-race in life. It is time for you to own what rightly belongs to you, and that is your right to become GREAT and live a great life. "The Corporate Hustle" will show you how to:

1. Recognize.
2. Plan.
3. Prepare.
4. Develop.
5. Understand.
6. Implement.
7. Share.
8. Conduct real business.

For the record, don't worry about your hardships, betrayals, pains, abuses, and rejection. They were all lessons to get you to this point in life. This ensured that you are able to recognize and understand the truth in what I am saying and be willing enough to use the principles and tools that I am giving you.

Your character, your creative abilities, your integrity, and your people skills are what's needed to build your best brand, which is YOU. However, you are required to be patient, you must persist, and you must persevere through, over, around, or under your stumbling blocks.

In and out of the corporate world, we are all winners! Although some may not feel that way due to their title, status, or pay grade; but, let me say this, our talents and creativity go far above our perceived limitations. Becoming a winner is all in how we think, as well as how we use our positive character traits to benefit others. Now, before I move on, let me clear the air...I have a lot of accomplishments under my belt; however, most of my superiors did not have degrees and doubled my pay grade. Therefore, I do not want anyone to become limited by fancy titles and pay grades because from my experience, my superiors had a mission in place, they believed in themselves, they believed in having a system in place, they never stop learning, and whatever they did not know, they found someone who did.

When we play to win, we do not settle for defeat! The rule is to revamp our plan, develop a system, find an expert to advise, and then re-approach. Once the re-approach is successful, we must mentor someone else to do the same! Does this really work? The answer is yes! Most individuals who own a business do not have degrees; they have an executable plan or vision in place. However, they are smart enough to get someone with a degree or specialty to implement their strategy or idea.

Hustle or no hustle, I am empowering individuals with this information to get them to understand when it comes down to doing business, we are all on an even playing field. The difference is our plans and processes...most take the easy way out by following a system that is set for them, and some will create their own. There is nothing wrong with either one, but I do encourage both until the income from the system we create for ourselves supersedes the one that is set for us.

When we are playing to win, there are a lot of elements in doing so. The first one is to know we are a winner. We were born a winner, or we would not be here at this present moment! Society has indeed contaminated us with doubt based upon the images they are feeding us or what we are feeding ourselves. However, if we know, understand, and apply the truth regarding our winning capabilities, then we will lead our field with a passion and originality that will keep us precisely on point with our next mission or our next move in life.

Secondly, once we embark upon our winning journey, we must become mindful of our environment. It is imperative that we weed out the dream killers because the negative energy can and will drain the life out of us. This is not about mistreating, degrading, or judging others; this is about choosing who is in our circle of positivity and who is not. We cannot subject ourselves to the atrocities of those who are set in their own ways, while not providing any form of positivity to sustain the connection. The goal is to lead with love, kindness, and compassion while moving on to those who are in need of what we have to offer. Even if someone thinks we feel as if we are better than them, keep in mind those are their thoughts; and, as long as we are treating people right, then we have nothing to worry about.

We cannot become a people-pleaser, due to the fact that people will play on our emotions to get us sidetracked from our mission or purpose in life. When we play with our integrity close to our chest, we can indeed protect ourselves from the influences of those who may want to play on our weaknesses. Of course, we all have strengths and weaknesses; however, we cannot allow others to use our shortcomings as a power play to drown out the winner from within. Keep in mind, a real winner will win to lose and lose to succeed as a completion of the cycle of life. This enables us to become more vibrant at winning and not bitter or competitive. It is through our element of winning that we are able to create other winners; and, if we are succeeding to create losers, then we must check our process, our ego, or our inner self-talk.

As a winner at heart, we cannot worry about what people think. We must become well aware of what we are thinking about ourselves at all times. Listen, the negative self-talk is a game-changer! It is for this reason, we must continue to do a positive checkup from the neck up to prevent any form of self-sabotage.

Thirdly, I create a vision board for myself to keep myself on target with my career, passions, hobbies, and goals. By doing so, I am able to keep myself balanced enough to win at living, while making a living, inspiring our inner passions, and having fun at the same time. Now, what I have found in corporate America, we become so consumed with a position, our next move, or how to get in good with the boss, where we forget about living a fulfilled life. When we go home, we take our job with us, and when we go to work, we block out everything and everyone that we hold dear to us. Real love cannot get in, and genuine love cannot get out; then at the end of the day when we are burned out or mentally exhausted, we are left wondering where we are going wrong.

In my personal experience, the time I took to block out the ones I loved while working; it took three times the amount of time to restore the damage or emotional trauma I caused. I thought they were sabotaging my career by calling me while at work; but what I realized, I was sabotaging myself with my insensitive people skills. When in all actuality, it only would take one extra minute of my time to answer the phone to show my loved ones I cared, or they were important. To tell the truth, I wasted more time lollygagging with those who could care less about my well-being or who were plotting my demise. In making all of my wrongs right, I realized it wasn't the time I spent on the phone that mattered; it was the quality of conversation I had that really made the difference.

Here is what I learned:
1. I learned the power of greetings.
2. I learned to listen.
3. I learned to ask fact-finding questions.
4. I learned not to respond with a solution until I am asked a question.
5. I learned how to schedule or set meetings for a specific conversation.
6. I have learned not to respond or react when I am engulfed with negative emotions.
7. I have learned how to think through my emotions while counteracting every negative feeling with a positive one.

What I have found is that once we master the connection to people using our people skills, we are better able to connect to our winning capabilities. What do I mean by winning capabilities, if we are already a winner? This is when we are able to take a negative situation and turn it into a positive regardless of how it may appear. Now, I must say, it takes a lot of training to master the skill of creating a win-win situation out of a negative one. However, throughout my journey, I have found that there is a lesson, blessing, and testing in all things. So, we must be willing to go into the classroom of life to extract wisdom.

Regardless of whether we are on a corporate or personal platform, we must be willing to extract the goodness of having a positive mental attitude. In corporate America, nothing is permanent, and everything is negotiable. Therefore, in order to play to win, we must always keep our resume or credentials updated whether or not we are in the market for a new position, business, or contract. This is merely good business, or better yet, professional etiquette for employees, business owners, and contractors.

If we have a desire to climb the corporate ladder, become a contractor, bidding for contracts, or gain new business, we must be on cue and ready to go at any given moment. Besides, with the flexibility of the internet, we are able to send our resumes or credentials to a person immediately upon request. Just make sure it is professional, as well as being in a simple, printable format.

One rule of thumb, we do not want to keep the person who has the potential to hire us waiting. Although, we must exhibit patience, but that may not be the case with the person who has more than one candidate waiting on that same position, bid, or contract. A first impression may be a lasting impression; so, do not drag your feet in this area. If you are not good at writing a personal, business, or credential resume, don't hesitate in having a professional organization write it, as well as keep it updated for you. In my opinion, it is worth the investment because credibility sales and believability will close the deal!

When being interviewed for a position, contract, bid, or new business, we must do our homework. We must know as much as possible about the company, so we can engage in effective communication. It is best to be proactive in identifying and understanding the vision of the company, as well as their products, services, or expectations. Here are a few other things we should know:

- As a part of our proactiveness, it is best to take notes when researching, while forming a list of questions to ask.
- Make sure we have our references readily available when asked.
- Dress professionally.
- Make sure we arrive early...it shows responsibility and timeliness.
- If we do not know the salary beforehand, do not appear desperate by asking during the interview. Usually, the interviewer will advise of the salary; if not, it is okay to ask after the job offer is made. If this is a bidding interview—make sure the bidding offer is adequately prepared and typed. Handwritten bids or proposals are

unacceptable! There are a lot of free apps and programs that will assist in developing a bid or proposal offer.

- I cannot say I do not get nervous during the interview, but I am going to say, remain calm.
- Focus on answering questions and making good eye contact, not on how nervous we are.
- Make sure we do not smoke or smell like smoke during an interview.
- Make sure our cell phone is on SILENT. It is disrespectful to have our phone ring or get a text message notification during an interview.

Thank the interviewer for their time. If we can give a small gift (i.e. pens, pendants, etc.) of appreciation, please do so. This is a phenomenal power play move, and it's not like we are buying them. It is basically using the Universal Law of Reciprocity. It may or may not work in getting the position, but it will get us remembered. Can you imagine how many people interview empty-handed? Let that not be you…as a part of *"The Corporate Hustle,"* we play to win.

CHAPTER 5

THE SOFT APPROACH

In corporate America, I encourage genuineness when communicating. Believability is essential in getting people to truly listen. We want our coworkers, clients, friends, and bosses to trust us, as well as our sense of judgment. When people are able to truly comprehend what we are saying and realize we genuinely care, they will open up. In my opinion, this technique works well in the sales industry. But, if they feel any form of inclination we are trying to fast-talk or manipulate them, they will erect walls.

I must say, it has been my fun-loving personality, as well as my skills that have created my staying power in the corporate arena. Yet, it was my superficial ego that has created a few pitfalls as well. When we are in the corporate world, it is not good to tell people they are wrong! It is our responsibility to provide solutions or questions to the wrongful elements of those who have the power to hire or fire us. I am not saying our superiors are not wrong from time-to-time; what I am saying is, we must find a different approach to making our superiors feel right without pointing the finger or calling them out. In the corporate world, this is one of the quickest ways to get blackballed. We never want to place our ego over our livelihood! I call this winning the battle but losing the war.

Listen, no one likes to be wrong, and no one wants to be humiliated; therefore, we must master our soft approach with questions and a sincere understanding. As we all know, our bosses do not have all the answers; however, as a corporate employee, it is our responsibility to make them feel as if they are the smartest thing since sliced bread! Is this deception? Maybe or maybe not, but it works! Would this be considered brown nosing? In my opinion, the answer is no. Brown nosing is the reactive, "Yes Sir Boss Mentality" and the soft approach is the proactive, "How can we win boss mentality." In my opinion, there is a difference. When we learn how to speak the language of our boss, we are better able to give them what they want, and they will be more than happy to provide us with what we want.

How can we give our boss what we don't have? As someone once told me, "Excuses are unacceptable, we have everything we need!" If we are in the position, then we have the skill; however, it must be sought after! We cannot discredit ourselves when we have not gone the extra mile in obtaining that in which is uncharted. Insecurity is a superficial distraction for other negative emotions to invade our mental or emotional space. If we give in, we will find that envy, jealousy, worry, and chaos will find its way into our corporate journey, causing us to second-guess ourselves when we should be elevating ourselves and those around us.

The ability to exude motivation, experience, and enthusiasm into what we do, say, or become takes time and patience. Once achieved, we will find that the feelings associated with greatness become contagious. Progressiveness in the developmental or the presentation phase will always create a hunger for more if we set the tone for the hunger. How can we set the tone for hunger? The answer is, "We need to ask questions," and "Provide the answers to those questions." Listen, we are problem solvers by nature; if we are being trusted to ask the right questions, we should be trusted enough to provide the answer or the solution. Once we are recognized as a problem-solver, it does build our level of value, as well as our marketability.

When we master the ability to trust ourselves, our thoughts, our intuition, our creativity, our ideas, etc.; we give ourselves the opportunity to represent an inner confidence that is permeated through the depths of the heart of those we encounter.

As a word to the wise, this is not an overnight process; it is a success journey that will try our patience. For me, this is where I learned the value of self-control. My self-control was not in controlling things; it was controlling myself and my reactions, which became the epitome of my *"Corporate Hustle"* in dealing with difficult people.

In *"The Corporate Hustle,"* you will encounter difficult people. It is not that they want to be difficult, it is a test to break you, bully you, or they may be trying to protect themselves. Regardless of their motive, do not let them see you sweat while exhibiting kindness, compassion, and positivity. Overreacting is one of the quickest ways to lose ground in corporate America! In the courtroom, attorneys go head to head and toe to toe to win their case; but, once that case is over, they are not archenemies—they are professionals, and they know how to get along.

As a rule of thumb in corporate America, "Business is Business!" You do not have to respond to ignorance, period! If you decide to respond, make your point positively, ask for an explanation, listen to them, and leave it alone. Do not respond in a negative demeanor, impatient demeanor, or a "know-it-all" demeanor. If you do, you have just given your power away because most of the time, difficult people are hurting, and they only want to be heard or understood.

Why does the soft approach work with difficult people? It works because we are emotional beings. Sincere compliments or understanding gestures work wonders on the human psyche. In my opinion, building rapport with people when they are not so pleasant or being able to start up conversations out of the blue gives us the ability to have a more significant impact. Plus, it will also give us the opportunity to narrow down their communicable language pattern or level to create a win-win situation. Lastly, if we want to master the power of negotiation, then we need to learn how to play by the rules of having good character; therefore, giving us leverage to deal with anyone.

CHAPTER 6

EMOTIONAL ANCHORING

Our level of influence is increased if we pay attention. It doesn't take a whole lot to hone in on what people are telling us. In my opinion, people will tell us exactly how they like being treated if we take the time to listen. Plus, humility, compassion, and kindness go a long way. When we use the element of communication to anchor emotionally, we give ourselves quite a bit of leverage when it comes down to our credibility.

What is emotional anchoring? It is when we are able to mirror the person we are communicating with while anchoring in with eye contact, our spoken words, our positive vibes, etc. It is often referred to as locking in or connecting, but for "*The Corporate Hustle*," our goal is to dig deep. Locking into or anchoring allows us to make an impact by listening, understanding, responding, asking the right questions, and providing solutions. In my opinion, the most significant communication problem is we do not listen to understand; we listen to reply. If we master listening to understand, we will always stay one step ahead of "*The Corporate Hustle!*"

Happy customers, employees, and family members make life's hustle a little easier; therefore, it is a good idea to master the emotional anchoring process. How do you become a powerful emotional anchor? The answer is, "Believe it!" If you are having a hard time believing it, then repeat this regularly: "I am the best emotional anchor alive." This is not a matter of tooting your own horn; it is about mastering the skills that God has given you to reach into the heart of man.

You have it because you were born with it. You simply need to reclaim it. How do you think you captured the heart of your parents? As a matter of fact, companies use testimonials from other customers to get you emotionally anchored to their products, right? This is something to think about—it happens all the time, and you do not recognize it. So, it is your time to use this same concept as a powerful tool of negotiation to leave a legacy with a positive impact. Soon enough, people will come to you confirming that you are an emotional anchor. Therefore, get it into your system and don't leave home without it.

When we invoke positive energy within people by speaking their mental or emotional language, people will begin to associate us with positive images, feelings, and thoughts by default. Even if they are prone to the negative, they will tend to back down if we are genuinely emotionally anchored with positivity. Bottom line, people are drawn to people who make them feel good about themselves, even in their wrongdoing. Nevertheless, right or wrong, good or bad, etc., we do not have the right to degrade or mistreat others. It is our responsibility to uplift, educate, build, inspire, and empower.

CHAPTER 7

THE CORPORATE HUSTLE

This book, "*The Corporate Hustle*" is not about materialism at all. I would say it is about hustlism in a good way. What is hustlism? Okay, I just created my own word here, but hustlism is about learning and understanding the grind of how to maximize our full potential, how to make the right connections, how to take action when necessary or when to stand down, and when to step up or when to step down.

My corporate hustle began with me learning how to believe in myself in spite of my humble beginnings. I grew up without a father to guide and direct me on my journey toward success. It was not as if I did not care that I did not have a male mentor; it was that I had to learn how to raise myself and take charge. When I saw others, who were not taking advantage of great opportunities, it would always take me back to my childhood of not having a father. In order for me to overcome the longing for a father figure, I became a father to others, including those who are reading this book.

For me, the hustle was real! I was not born with a silver spoon in my mouth. But I made a promise to myself; I would create my own spoon to ensure my children would never have to go through what I endured on my journey.

The goal of *"The Corporate Hustle"* is to inspire others to develop a positive mindset, thinking their way into greatness with no regrets. I firmly believe once we change the way we think, our life will change, guaranteed. For this reason, I am here to become the mentor to hustle the up and coming into their lifelong passions. The one thing I longed for was the self-assurance of knowing my legacy of my corporate hustle will live on. With this book, I have achieved a life-long goal of sharing information that will last a lifetime.

In the corporate world, we are trained to appear confident about everything, even if we don't know or understand certain things. However, what I have found is, if we pretend to know everything, people will stop helping us, or they will not answer the questions that need to be answered. For me, as a rule of thumb, if I don't understand something, I ask questions. Throughout my journey, it was asking the right questions that allowed me to become an EXPERT in my field.

Now, I am sharing the power of becoming the pilot of our future, and once we make minor changes while becoming an expert in our field, our inner born autopilot will kick in. If my lead is followed, it will direct us on a journey of greatness that will supersede what we could have ever imagined, while our creativity takes the wheel in creating a zeal that is unmatched.

However, the hustle of life does require us to set our gifts, talents, creativity, or skills in motion. We cannot sit around with the tools of greatness and not do anything with them; we must use them. If not, they will get a little rusty, and we do not want that to happen.

What I have found throughout my hustle is that most of us do not have a clue about our passions in life. Although we are in the corporate arena, we are really treading the mill for the paycheck, knowing that we are somehow missing the mark. If this is happening, there is no reason to feel alone...it is happening more than we could care to imagine. Nevertheless, it is imperative that we take some time out to do a little self-discovery to determine what brings joy to the depths of our soul. This is not about who is the smartest, who is the most intellectual, who has the most degrees, or who is the most qualified. It's about who is the most transparent, who is the most teachable, who is the most understandable, who is the most pliable, who is the most disciplined, and who is the most driven.

Corporations are driven by plans, systems, concepts, rules, and strategies. If we have a desire to fit in or to become sought after, one must become a person who thinks on his or her feet with integrity. Trustworthiness is essential in becoming someone who is prided on being the one with the conceptual knowledge of strategic building. The originality in our thinking process does give us leverage in the world of business, and it does give us a unique platform when dealing with our inner passion as well.

Fitting into the vision of a company is essential in building a vision of our own. If we cannot deal with being told what to do; more than likely, we may be dealing with a personal disciplinary issue that must be rectified immediately. This is not about being able to keep a job, because there are a lot of unruly, undisciplined, and hateful people who have been on the job for many years; however, in my opinion, in most cases that is where their level of progression stops. They are able to work for someone, but they are not able to build, sustain, or maintain their own company. Nevertheless, I am convinced after completing this book, this will not be you, right?

In order to increase our access in corporate America, we have to find a way to become inspirational and motivational. We do not need to be perfect to have an impact! It does not matter if people are smarter, more educated, more experienced, etc.; all we need to do is figure out what language they are speaking, then step up, step down, or remain on that level. If they are on the same playing field, no problem. If we think for a minute, we cannot maneuver in such a manner, then think again.

When we learn how to speak to people on their level, we will find the ability to lock in on their needs, wants, and desires are much easier. Why is it much easier? It is really straightforward; they will tell us! Once they begin to feed us the information regarding the need, want, or desire, we are able to paint a crystal-clear picture in our mind's eye. How do we master this tool? First, we must acknowledge that we have the ability to do it. Secondly, we must begin practicing using this skill. Thirdly, we must master the ability to connect by asking the right questions to determine the language, as well as the playing field. For example, this is like playing sports:

1. We determine which game we are playing—basketball, soccer, baseball, golf, etc.
2. We must line up with the rules and boundaries of the game because they are all different depending upon the choice of sport.
3. We must RESPECT the game.
4. We then connect to the game. Keep in mind, if we do not exhibit respect prior to connecting, we will miss the mark. We cannot truly connect to what we do not respect.
5. We play to win. Keep in mind this is not a competition; this is about learning the power that is encapsulated in speaking the language of the people we come in contact with.

When we say we cannot relate to something or someone, it is an excuse! We all have an imagination, we all have compassion, and we all have the ability to love. In my opinion, not being able to relate is a choice. In the corporate arena, we must be able to connect to others. Our people skills will make us or break us…we cannot get on the playing field, have a temper-tantrum, and then say we cannot relate. Find a way!

When we are playing to win, we cannot limit ourselves with watered down excuses we don't even believe. I know about this all too well. I made excuses about my behavior for many years, until one day, the hustle became my reality. I finally realized I was in it to win it, and I was not going to allow excuses to hold me back. Here is what I used to find my way:

H-Hearing with Humility.
U-Understanding with Precision.
S-Sympathizing with Kindness, Compassion, and Love.
T-Teaching the Power of Development.
L-Learning more to create an impact of effectiveness.
E-Elevating through the mentoring process.

This will help you beyond what you can ever imagine. All I need for you to do is share it once you master it. The Law of Reciprocity works for all; besides, sharing helps us to lock in wisdom.

I am a member of various organizations that assist with my personal development. However, the one I gained the most from happens to be a non-profit, National Sales Network organization (NSN). As a member of NSN organization, I took advantage of their annual conference and sponsored Career Fair. This conference provides a platform for their sponsors to hire high caliber sales professionals. Along with their industry-led presentations, workshops, and debates, the local chapters from around the U.S. participate in personal development with ongoing training programs. This provided a high-level networking platform for me, and it will do the same for you. Rest assured, you will find me there! I encourage you to check them out; the website is www.salesnetwork.org.

CHAPTER 8

SAFEGUARDING OUR LIMITS

Our self-expression has everything to do with who we are, our direction in life, our goals, as well as the level of our creativity. If we can find a way to eliminate the distractions, we will find our level of expression will change. Changing for the better is the ultimate goal; therefore, it is imperative that we take into account the type of distractions we are exposed to. Keep in mind, we all have positive and negative distractions whether we like it or not.

As a part of *"The Corporate Hustle,"* our goal is to get rid of the negative and maximize the positive. Now, the question is, "How can we have a positive distraction?" A positive distraction keeps us from engaging in people, places, things, or events that are not conducive to our well-being or counterproductive in the direction we are taking in our personal or professional lives.

The true corporate arena gives us an opportunity to showcase or downplay our skills based upon our ultimate goal or the ulterior motives of the people we are dealing with within the organization. If for some reason, our talents are being suppressed due to the envy or jealousy of our peers, it may be a viable option to seek another position, find another job, or start a company of our own. There is nothing like feeling under-utilized, deprived, or mistreated because we are skilled, gifted, or talented in areas our peers are not. When a company allows employees to sabotage other employees intentionally, it creates a domino effect of frivolous behaviors to emotionally or mentally traumatize others. Is this fair? Absolutely not.

In my opinion, major corporations must become very careful about hiring employees that bully, discriminate, degrade, harass, or violate the privacy of other employees. Intentionally creating a hostile environment to weed out the unwanted individuals is an atrocity, because there are times when we could be weeding out our miracle in disguise.

Hiring employees in a corporation who exhibits this sort of behavior does subject them to justifiable lawsuits if this sort of behavior is tolerated. Furthermore, when we are in *"The Corporate Hustle,"* we must make it our business not to engage in this sort of behavior due to the fact that our blessings are always in disguise. In so many words, our blessings will never appear as such…it will present itself as something we would reject. For this reason, we must be cautious about our behavior, while building a repertoire of good character traits that will keep our elements of favor in high effect.

When I talk about the hustle, I am definitely not speaking about hustling people…everyone deserves equal rights, respect, and fair treatment. I am referring to working hard, setting goals, developing systems, while becoming the best version of self. Periodically, take one of your associates out to lunch with you to brainstorm. You will be surprised at how you can bounce ideas off each other.

As a part of corporate wisdom, you and your superiors, as well as your coworkers, are business associates, not friends! Building work relationships and building personal friendships are not the same; although, there is a thin line between the two. Do not cross them and do not allow them to cross them as well. Most would think becoming personal friends with superiors and coworkers would be a smart move, but it is NOT. This is not the foundation for a successful career, but I must admit, it is a substitute for talent!

Nevertheless, business is business, and your personal life is personal. I promise, if you work hard on building your positive people skills, creativity, and talent more than you fraternize on the job with friends, you will always stay ahead of the game. Keep in mind, this is not a license to mistreat others; you are still required to be kind, communicate effectively, smile, handle your business, and help them in any way possible. But as long as you are at the same company, set limits!

In graduate school, we discussed the PIE Theory; this stands for Performance-Image-Exposure. This is one theory I will never forget. I started applying this theory to my life in 1999, and it has not stopped working for me yet. So, let me share this with you:

P stands for **PERFORMANCE**. About ten percent of your advancements and promotions depend on your performance. This is doing your job, participating, attendance, or doing what you are required to do.

I stands for **IMAGE**. About thirty percent is about your grooming. Being neat, clean, smelling fresh, and wearing the normal clothing you see your managers wearing.

E stands for **EXPOSURE**. About sixty percent is how well people like you, being known as the go-to person, and knowing the SWOT (strengths, weaknesses, opportunities, and threats) analysis of yourself and the individuals you interact with at work.

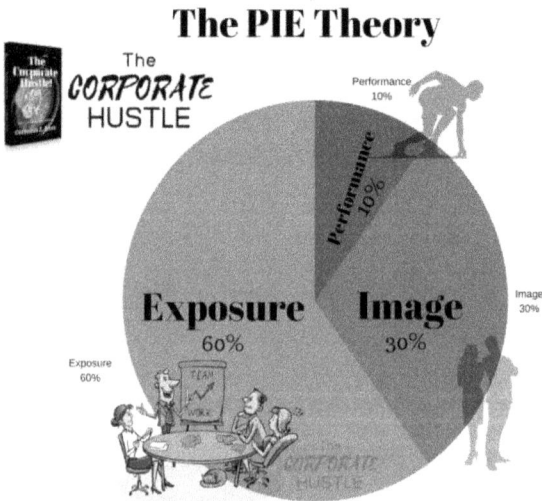

The PIE Theory

The PIE Theory says nothing about being friends; it is referring to Exposure as being the vital aspect of rising to the top. Now with that being said, if you are somehow an attention seeker, it is good to know your strengths, weaknesses, opportunities, and threats. This is commonly referred to as the SWOT analysis.

A SWOT analysis can be used for you, companies, products, places, or an industry. It encompasses specifying the objective of a person, venture, or project, then identifying the internal and external factors that are positive and negative in order to achieve the overall goal. The analysis will help you to become effectively aware! Aware of what? It helps you to become aware of you, as well as your environment to overcome and work through any and all obstacles or codependences. Here is a sample layout:

SWOT ANALYSIS

S STRENGTHS	W WEAKNESSES
1. 2. 3. 4. 5.	1. 2. 3. 4. 5.
O OPPORTUNITIES	T THREATS
1. 2. 3. 4. 5.	1. 2. 3. 4. 5.

Once you have listed your strengths, weaknesses, opportunities, and threats, you are then able to ask yourself the what, when, where, how, and why questions for a better understanding of your positive and negative attributes, how you can improve, and how you are able to contribute to an overall common goal.

CHAPTER 9

THE POWER OF TIME

The shortsightedness of time has been around for centuries, as well as the saying, "Timing is everything." Now, if timing is really everything, why are so many of us missing out without realizing it? In my opinion, there are times when we miss out due to laziness, procrastination, or the lack of understanding. Nonetheless, if we are missing out on our greatness, I would consider this a non-conducive playing field that must be rectified immediately.

When it comes down to managing our time, we must take into account how time fits into our character. Anyone can alter their personality to open doors; however, the goal of *"The Corporate Hustle"* is to keep the doors open. The best way I have found to win at keeping doors open is being able to manage my time effectively. If a person is late all the time, there may be a hidden character defect they need to resolve quickly.

When we do not respect our time or the time of others, we will find we make a lot of excuses. Yes, excuses! We cannot pass the buck in the hustle; we must own it. Our astuteness of time is vital in our pursuit of success; if not, we will procrastinate, we will miss deadlines, we will do our work at the last minute, or we will get into a routine of rushing. When we find ourselves out of character with our time, we will discover we may become a little condescending when people point it out to us, especially when we are in denial of our truth.

In corporate America, we look for timeliness. If we think for a minute we can defy time, think again. If we miss our moment in our personal or professional life, do we actually believe we can regain that specific moment in time? The answer is no. Although we may get a second chance at a different time, the previous moment is over, and we are forced to move on with or without our permission. Therefore, it behooves us to maximize every moment to ensure we are not missing out due to our untimeliness.

Believe it or not, our integrity is wrapped in our ability to respect time as well. Although most take the essence of time for granted, it is the number one determining factor of trust, the reason for distrust, as well as the level of disappointment. When we feel as if the world is centered around us, we will get into the mindset of thinking that time is centered around us as well; when in all actuality, we are centered around time.

The value of time is a hidden treasure that most overlook because they feel as if they are in control. I do agree, we have some form of control over self, but we cannot control time! It is for this reason, we must learn how to MANAGE it effectively.

Here is a little secret, if you want people to respect you, respect their time, period. Leading your field in GREATNESS is led by:

1. Learning the rules of business engagement.
2. How well you manage your time.
3. Your Positive Mental Attitude.
4. Your positive character traits.
5. Your level of humility.
6. Your level of loyalty.

We can spend years talking about doing something, but if we do not carve out the time to do it, our words do not have bonding power or believability. In order to speak things into reality, we must be able to form a trustworthy relationship with time. Better yet, if time is on our side, it will provoke our conscience with an element of favor nudging us when to move, as well as the instincts to recoil if necessary.

For those who properly manage their time, they usually have less time to take things personally. As a matter of fact, they have even less time for foolery, and they are quick to move on if there is no added benefit or if it causes them to become distracted. When you are a good steward over your time, you are less likely to feel at the mercy of those who allow time to pass them by.

We are selfish by nature, and we are unselfish by our properly governed characterizable instincts. If we are not in touch with time, we may overlook our selfish nature because we are so engulfed in what we want, and not what is best. According to the Universal Law of seed, time, and harvest, we have phases in our lives where the element of time will bridge the gap between our seed and our harvest. Now with this three-fold binding principle, we cannot put the cart before the horse; and, we must respect proper protocol regardless of our self-governed reasonings.

Excuses for our negative behaviors or actions are indeed a good success blocker. How do we know if negativity is causing us to make excuses?

1. When we have unresolved hurts, pain, or trauma.
2. When we have unmet or ungoverned needs.
3. When we are basing our worth from material wants or gain.
4. When we are paralyzed with fear.
5. When we have unrecognizable or unresolved hang-ups.
6. When we are continually using others for our benefit.
7. When we have ulterior motives.
8. When we have hidden insecurities.
9. When our ego is super inflated.
10. When we are easily ashamed of people for being who they are.

As we move through life, we will find everything we do, say, or become is based upon some element of time. For the most part, time is often taken for granted because we are all guilty of wasting it as opposed to maximizing it. But my question is, "We all have 24 hours in a day, why are some people running out of time every day?" I understand things come up and our lives are hectic; but, running out of time daily means our management process is a little off. Who am I to judge, right? Beyond a shadow of a doubt, I am guilty of this from time-to-time; but for the most part, I have a system set up for myself that will assist in the time-management process.

Here is what I do with my time-management plan for my Corporate Hustle:

- I create a plan of action or a timeline for almost everything.
- I plan my tomorrow at the end of today because it may incorporate tasks from that day. Overlapping responsibilities are okay, as long as I get them done.
- I start and end my day with prayer, giving THANKS for the time that I have. I also BLESS my day in the morning, and I BLESS my night in the evening.
- I develop a system of how I conduct business.
- If I need to incorporate a strategy or some form of negotiation, here is where I will insert it.
- I make sure I understand my "WHY" of what I am doing…the "Just Because" is not an option when we are running out of time daily. I save the "Just Because" for my free day on Saturday, where I am open to doing whatever I want, whenever I want, and for whatever reason I want.

- I keep my mind centered on the present, not the past or the future until my task or goals are complete. My future goals are already planned; therefore, I cannot spend time on those goals until the appointed time that I have set for myself—I just take notes and sort them out then.

Time has given us the opportunity to create some form of balance in our lives, while it is our responsibility to do the legwork in setting the structure for it. If we fail to realize its value, then life will toss us to and fro, keeping us at an apparent loss of valuable time. Just remember, time is a tool, and it can also become our kryptonite if misappropriated.

CHAPTER 10
BUDGETING AND WEALTH BUILDING

When embarking upon the journey into corporate America, we must learn how to manage and save money, period. If we are working and spending every dime that we have, then we may find ourselves upside down in a pile of debt just to keep up with the Joneses. In my opinion, there are so many ways to cut cost, whether it is with the way in which we spend money, with our home, with our vehicle, on our groceries, on our wardrobe, etc. There are so many ways to save money; we just need to find them.

As a matter of fact, if we are spending unnecessary money or accumulating credit card debt to keep up a superficial image, we are totally out of order. Plus, in today's economy, we can make it very tough on ourselves, as well as our families when we overspend to the point of suffering. Eating out, treating ourselves to a $4 cup of coffee, excessive snacks, etc. on a daily basis can put a dent in our pockets, as well as put our health at risk. If we take the time to cook healthy meals, take our lunch to work, and eat healthy snacks, we will save money; in addition, we can safeguard our health and unnecessary visits to the doctor.

When we indulge in the unbudgeted splurging, it creates a form of undisciplined behaviors that contributes to our lack of self-control. However, if splurging makes someone feel better, it is best to create a budgeted account for that behavior.

Regardless of whether or not we choose to put ourselves on a budget, there are some who are downright cheap, and there are some who are downright frugal. What I have found throughout my *"Corporate Hustle"* is most people do not understand the difference. A stingy person does not like to share; they live like a miser. They are always on the take— getting something for nothing. They use people to get what they want and very rarely give to those who are in need. Most often, they are very critical, negative, and judgmental, condemning those who appear less than them.

A frugal person is cost conscience; they are fully aware of:

1. What they are spending.
2. Why they are spending.
3. How they are spending.
4. Where they are spending.
5. When they are spending.
6. Who they are spending with.

Bottom line, a frugal person questions their money. In my opinion, there is nothing wrong with knowing where our money is going. We cannot be clueless about our spending practices. A frugal person will search for deals; they try not to pay full price for anything. They buy what they need, and "Budget Spend" on their wants. What is "Budget Spend?" It is when we spend from a specific budget such as:

1. A grocery budget.
2. A personal item budget.
3. A vacation budget.
4. A hobby budget.
5. A car maintenance budget.
6. A house maintenance budget.

I am proud of being frugal; I love looking for deals! Why spend more when we do not have to? I get at least three estimates on everything, playing each seller or contractor against the next for the lowest price. When searching for the best deals on luxury vehicles, I target men going through divorces, where they need to liquidate assets quickly. Actually, I purchased my last car from my Ophthalmologist, who was offloading assets for cash prior to his divorce.

My frugality traits have given me leverage on my job as well. Management has never questioned my expenses because I am always under budget. I am often asked to discuss my tactics and techniques of curtailing cost in a training module at the yearly kick-off meeting. When speaking at company events, my infamous slogan is, "I treat the company's money like my own; and, the thought of going to jail scares me."

What I am advocating is becoming a good steward over what we are blessed to have. Here is how I make my Corporate Hustle work for me:

- I set aside a certain amount of money each paycheck for inevitable incidentals such as car maintenance, tires, clothing, etc.
- I clip coupons on items I use the most. I will elaborate on this a little later.
- I buy in bulk. It's a great way to save on groceries. I keep all the tissue, dish liquid, etc. in the attic until needed
- I do not waste electricity...I turn off any unused lights, and I set my thermostat at a specific temperature.
- I do not waste water. I brush my teeth with a cup of water until I'm done and then turn on the water.
- I shop at the mall, thrift stores, or garage sales for bargains, as well as rare finds. As a hobby, I sell on Amazon or Ebay. What a great feeling when the funds hit my Paypal account. I recall one beat-up metal toy fire truck I purchased for $2.50, it went for $1500 to a rare toy collector on Amazon!
- I barter my expertise. This is where we are able to trade our services with others for free or for a deep discount.

Create a budget and keep a list of what is being spent. In order to maneuver effectively throughout life, we must learn how to commit to cutting cost. I have an excel spreadsheet where I forecast a monthly budget for allotted expenses, which aligns with my take-home pay. Also, next to my forecast columns are actual spend columns. At the end of the month, the forecast is subtracted from the actuals, and if an overage, it is allotted to my investment accounts and disposable income. It may take a few months to fine-tune this process; but eventually, you get comfortable with it and reap the benefits.

Although I am very frugal, you would never suspect that I am, unless you ask me about what works for me when it comes down to my finances. I recall being asked by the person I was dating at the time, "Have you spent your clothing budget for the month?" I took a moment to think about it...then I realized that I had not used my clothing budget for about four months. She was eyeing a Louis Vuitton purse. I immediately pulled out my American express and purchased it. I was able to do that because it was within my budget. So, you see, I buy nice things as long as it is within my budgeted circumference.

Most people do not realize that budgeting is a part of wealth building. In my opinion, this is why they keep spending on liabilities as opposed to assets. As a part of "The Corporate Hustle," it is always best to get into building wealth the most logical way. The first thing I did was to maximize my investments and benefits with the company I am employed. Most corporations have at least a 401K, Flexible Spending Account and there are still a few with a Pension plan. The company matches what you put in up to a certain amount, which is **FREE** money to you. Therefore, get with HR and set up an appointment with the investment company being utilized at your job.

Here is the secret…with the extra funds from budgeting, purchasing in bulk, Amazon sales, paying myself 10% of my paycheck and other additional funds, I have them going to Mutual Funds (varied with major stocks down to penny stocks) and Money Market accounts (liquid cash paying more than regular Savings or CDs pending the market). This can be done through Fidelity and TD Ameritrade; as a matter of fact, this is where I have my Financial Mentor/Planner.

The key is to find someone you genuinely trust to do this for you. How do you find someone you trust with your money? I have a few sayings, "My deals are not based on trust; they are based on unprecedented verification!" "Trust, but verify." The three Financial Mentors/Planners I do business with, hated me at first. I had them review their personal credit reports, as well as their investment portfolio with me, before doing business. I would not let someone with poor credit or without a favorable personal investment portfolio manage my money, and you should not either. There are many companies that do not hire employees with poor credit, and the company I work for is one of them. There is a money management concern with providing an individual with an expense account who has poor credit. Keep in mind, if you have a little hiccup with your credit, there are programs to help improve or build your credit.

Regardless of whether you are in *"The Corporate Hustle"* or whether you are getting hustled; good credit, bad credit, or no credit, get yourself on a budget and open a few investment accounts. The minimum to open a TD Ameritrade account is about $1500, and you can manage it yourself. You must master what is coming in, as well as what is going out. I am here to help you get into the perfect mindset of abundant living where all things work together for your good. Here are a few ways I created additional income for myself:

- Once my car was paid off, I continued to pay myself the monthly payments for two additional years. I took the car payment amount, and I place it into my investment accounts.

- I used my ability and passion for working on cars to partner up with an individual with a car dealer's license. I purchased cars from the auction and sold them; while using the profits for investments as opposed to spending the profits.

- The company I worked for paid for my graduate degree. However, while in graduate school, I took out student loans. I put the loan money for each semester for two years into my investments. After completing graduate school, I paid the loans off, while still yielding a profit.

- I promised to elaborate on couponing. So, about five years ago, I was in the grocery store, and I heard a lot of customers complaining about how cheap this lady was. She was holding up the line couponing; she had no sense of shame in what she was doing. As my curiosity was peaked, my personality pushed me to inquire about how she purchased about $400.00 worth of merchandise for approximately $30.00. After helping her load her products into her van, I found that she will not pay more than $1.00 for an item using coupons. Her goal was to get everything for free. This person took my hustling to a WHOLE different level. She came out of corporate America for a time of unparalleled creative freedom. Also, she has written several self-help books which contributed to my wealth building journey; and, to this day, she remains one of my best friends.

Implementing the programs such as budgeting, 401K, Mutual Funds, Money Market, and purchasing a few rental properties enabled me the opportunity to become a millionaire within 5 years. If I can do this, you can too. Listed below are a few stocks that I have in my funds that you can start with:

"Bank of America (BAC), Union Pacific Corp (UP), TJ Maxx (TJX), Anheuser Bush (BUD), Nike (NKE), Cormedix (CRMD), United Technologies (UTX), Groupon (GRPN), Costco (COST), Facebook (FB), Telsa (TSLA), Fortress Investment (FIG), Netflix (NFLX), Spotify (SPOT), CSX Corp (CSX), Burlington Northern Sante Fa (BRK-B), ExxonMobil (XOM), UnitedHealth Group (UNH), Shell (RDS.A), Pepsico (PEP), Walmart (WMT), CVS (CVS), Walgreens (WBA)."

When we are committed to saving money and investing, we will become mindful of the things that most people take for granted. These are just a few ways to get the ball rolling on saving and investing.

CHAPTER 11

SELF-GROWTH VS. INNER-GROWTH

In corporate America, the lack of self-esteem has a way of negatively impacting our effectiveness. But the funny thing about low self-esteem, we are conditioned to think it resides only with the uneducated, poor, or someone with a lower socio-economic upbringing. And this is so far from the truth. We all suffered from low self-esteem at some point in our lives. If you have not, then live a little longer; it will knock on your door. The key is not holding onto and knowing how to deal with it.

Listen, there is some form of insecurity residing in the areas we feel the most challenged—but it's okay, we simply need to learn the power of redirecting our energy and balancing our lives. What I have found is, most people tend to avoid the insecure areas while overcompensating in the areas they are confident. Now in order to maximize this area, we must be willing to confront our insecurities, asking the right fact-finding questions to understand the core of that negative feeling. Once we understand it, we are then able to do something about it, while replacing it with something positive. There is no reason to sacrifice your personal power when you have the opportunity to create a win-win situation.

You are the best you that you have, and there is no reason to feel incomplete…besides the weakest areas of your life are usually your blessing in disguise. Therefore, don't misinterpret what you are feeling, get to the bottom of it, building a level of confidence that will put your naysayers in a state of awe.

There are a lot of people succeeding by doing little or no research, they do not have a business plan, they do not have a mission statement, they do not have a sense of direction, they tread the mill every day with little or no marketing, and they do not have a lot of things, but their customer service is impeccable. How successful would this company become if they had the business essentials in place?

Here is a better question, "How is this company different from a company that has all that is needed to do business; but treats their employees awful and their customers even worse?" Who wins in this situation? From my perspective, business ethics trumps what we have written on paper!

Life skills are now the new developmental approach with major corporations; however, to get their employees to take advantage of self-improvement or life-improvement can be challenging. Why is it so challenging? There is so much power play in corporate America, where most think they know it all or they have arrived base upon their position or pay grade. To add insult to injury, they turn around and treat others like they were treated on their way up the ladder of success.

In my opinion, that should make us want to treat others better; however, the ego does prevent a lot of people from doing a check-up from the neck up. More importantly, the same way we are looking down on people, there are those who are looking up to us as well; therefore, we must always become cognizant of our behavior and attitude.

Self-growth is a vital aspect required when attempting to maximize our full potential. Of course, we all understand the developmental process is natural, but what we fail to understand is that our inner-growth is a conscious process that must be cultivated. If not, we will find ourselves taking two steps forward, and three steps back, due to the emotional hiccups that we think are natural or caused by others when they are not.

Regardless of whether or not we are in *"The Corporate Hustle,"* we all have some sort of skill, and we are all good at something. There are times when we may have to search for it; but in all reality, it's there. As a matter of fact, there are also times when we may have to engage in some form of self-development in order to narrow down our good traits. Which is absolutely okay…we are designed to learn and grow—there is no reason to feel bad about going back into the classroom.

"The Corporate Hustle" encapsulates our innate ability to work on, work at, or work through the desires and goals we have set for ourselves. We cannot fear working, and we cannot allow our mind to become idle. From my experience, mental idleness leaves room for our mind to become the devil's playground.

This is where our mind becomes bombarded with all types of thoughts that create unnecessary emotional sabotage. For the record, mental rest and mental idleness are different—mental rest is resting the mind or when we allow ourselves to hear our thoughts, where we are in control. Mental idleness is laziness or slothfulness of the mind, where we are not in control of our thoughts, nor do we care. This is when we allow our mind to run wild with negative, destructive thoughts that create the same mirror emotions that contribute to bad choices and many regrets.

Keep in mind, personal or professional development is an ongoing process; better yet, it is lifelong. In my opinion, the developmental process increases our level of awareness, and it also gives us the ability to own our truth about where we are, as well as where we are going.

It is commonly said, "We become what we think about," "As a man thinketh, so is he," and "We are the product of our thoughts." But, what about the lost thoughts? What about the ideas that are not thought of yet? What do we do with those? Absolutely nothing. It is imperative that we stay in the now with our thoughts; by doing so, it gives us the ability to correct them. Besides, with the correction of our right now, thoughts can change the trajectory of the future ones; therefore, don't waste time. Plus, if we lose a thought, we can tell it to come back; if it doesn't, then don't worry about it. More than likely, that thought will reappear when our mind is at rest or when it is triggered by something or someone.

In corporate America, our thoughts and what comes out of our mouth will make or break us. As a matter of fact, in *"The*

Corporate Hustle," we must make sure we are setting a positive guard over our thoughts, our actions, as well as our mouth. Under no circumstances do we make important decisions when we are emotional or under some form of duress. If we need to take a breather, take it. If we need to pray, pray. Whatever must be done to step away from decision making at this point, do it. As I stated earlier, the hustle is real; however, it does not negate the fact that we must be able to think through our decisions.

The molding force of our character resides in what we think, in addition to our manifested thoughts turned into an action, reaction, behavior, habit, or some form of communication. It is for this reason, the renewing of our mind on a moment-by-moment basis is extremely important. It only takes a fraction of a second for our thoughts to go to the left or for us to get mentally caught up. Some may laugh about it, but we must reel in our thoughts constantly because they are directly linked to our emotions.

CHAPTER 12

THE CORPORATE LEVEL OF PMA

Having a Positive Mental Attitude (PMA) is vital, but does it work? The answer is yes. I am going to share how it worked for me, and how we can always keep the ball in our court even when we are not getting what we want. Having a positive outlook is vital in the corporate arena, as well as in our personal lives.

It takes a willingness on our behalf to connect to the positive side of the developmental process of our PMA. Once we master the elements of staying on the positive side of the spectrum, then it becomes more manageable. Nonetheless, this is one skillset that we must work for, work at, work on, and work toward. The goal is to operate at our highest potential; so, we will continue to be a work-in-progress because we change, things change, people change, companies change, etc. Therefore, we cannot get locked in a box when it comes down to our PMA status because what worked yesterday, may not work today. So, we must be ready at all times geared with awareness, proactiveness, and connectivity—if we leave these ingredients out, we may miss the mark. Here is how I make it work for me:

- Awareness—I become aware of the person, place, situation, circumstance, or event. That means I pay attention to the little small things that most people take for granted.
- Proactiveness—I listen, understand, and assess in order to take care of a need, question, or desire before it is needed or asked for, with the elements of love, kindness, genuineness, and compassion.
- Connectivity—I connect to others based upon their individual needs. I speak their language emotionally, mentally, and physically. I can only do this by first becoming aware and then being proactive to make the connection to become effective.

This is how I make PMA work for me, and it will work for those who are willing to go the extra mile. However, the goal is to become EFFECTIVE!

Due to our subconscious programming based upon our background, experiences, and upbringing, we will find that our perception may vary from one person to the next. However, it is our responsibility to learn how to connect to others without violating their space or disrespecting their way of thinking.

With our PMA, we cannot come off as arrogant or overbearing; we must become authentic with our approach or conveyance of what we have to offer. From my personal experience, people will tend to reject a know-it-all individual, but they will open up to someone who has a humble and meek spirit.

A PMA gives us the ability to overcome the negative with something positive. The mental process of positivity starts with the way we think, the thoughts we feed ourselves, and what we allow our inner chatter to speak to us. Although most of us only focus on the thoughts and affirmations of our PMA, what about the internal chatter, we cannot tell anyone about? In my opinion, this is the inner hustle that must become tamed; if not, this is where the two faces of our personality will manifest. Plus, in the corporate world, we do not want to get labeled as being two-faced, a backbiter, or a dream killer.

As we all know, we are human, and we are subjected to err on occasion; however, we must become mindful of our reputation, as well as our ability to treat others with love and respect. Of course, challenges will come and go, but it is not good to be on an emotional rollercoaster in the workplace. It is not a good look, and it could become disturbing to others who are not sure of our mental or emotional state; therefore, it is imperative that we fine-tune our inner struggles or seek professional help. Regardless of where we are in life, it is okay to receive professional counseling to develop our PMA if there is some underlying hurt or trauma that is preventing our positivity from coming forth.

When dealing with our PMA, it does not incorporate our excuses, denials, fears, or unresolved character flaws. Our

PMA is one area of development; our excuses are another, and so on. We cannot think for a minute that once we master our PMA, we are done. Our PMA is designed to keep our thoughts in check, but it does not fix the weak or broken elements of our inner man or character. We must use our PMA as a tool and not a solution. For example, if we are dealing with fear, we must find the origin of our fear, understand the "Why" of it, and find the solution. Once it is resolved, then when fear creeps up in this particular area again, we will then use our PMA as a tool to counteract the thought, feeling, emotion, or behavior.

It is imperative that we face our inner struggles head-on. By denying what needs to be faced creates emotional triggers that could appear at any given moment. In addition, it prolongs our healing process creating a systematic process of déjà vu. When history keeps repeating itself, it is an indication that we are not learning the lessons in this particular area; and, déjà vu of our yesterday's mistakes or traumas will not cease until they are faced, or the lessons are learned.

In order to move to the next level in life, we must extract the wisdom that is hidden on our level. If not, empty elevation leaves a little cushion to bounce back after a fall. In so many words, in the corporate world, once we are promoted to the next level, we need staying power! Learning, knowing, growing, and sharing contributes to our staying power; but it is exhibiting positive characteristics and a Positive Mental Attitude that make us EFFECTIVE.

In our personal or professional life, positive thoughts attract positive people, situations, and outcomes. Whereas negative thoughts attract likewise. Nevertheless, the best thing about it, we have a choice! We are able to choose our mindset regardless of what others think, say, or do. How do we know if we are a negative person or have negative character traits? Here are a few indicators:

- If we are a constant complainer.
- If we are a constant faultfinder.
- If we think and believe the worst about life and people.
- If we believe that we or others cannot get anything right.
- If we continuously belittle others.
- If we hate everything and everyone.
- If we constantly look for the negative.
- If we are always picking fights or engaging in chaos.
- If we cannot congratulate others.
- If we have a problem saying, please and thank you.
- If we are mean and hateful.
- If we hold grudges.
- If we are unforgiving or unmerciful.

With this in mind, we are all a work-in-progress; this list is not designed to make anyone feel bad or discount our right to be who we are. These are just a few indicators that alert us of negative energy, which can be changed at any given moment. Even if our emotion, trauma, or pain is real, we will always have the opportunity to shift the energy to a positive vibe.

When I am faced with a negative situation, circumstance, or person, I simply change my perception. The way we perceive people, places, and things determine how we feel if we are not in the know! Professional manipulation or stimulation is here to stay, and if we are not aware of how to perceive in a positive light, it then becomes easy for the negative to slip in without us realizing what is taking place. As a result, we must safeguard how we perceive while incorporating it with love, kindness, peace, compassion, understanding, and mercy. I have personally found that it does the perception quite well, and it makes it much easier to answer our "Why" questions.

Always remember, once we eliminate our old beliefs, habits, thoughts, actions, and reactions, we are then able to attract and keep the people, places, and things we desire the most. Keep in mind, all the answers to our solutions during the hustle are already within. So, stop focusing on the problem and start understanding the "Why" and maximize the opportunities that are hidden in plain sight.

CHAPTER 13

THE POWER OF OUR WHY

Regardless of where we are in life, we all have questions, and we all have our doubts. If we all have questions and doubts, how do we get the answers? Throughout my corporate journey, I have found that most of our problems are already answered; we simply need to learn how to ask the right question. Once we answer the "Why" portion of our problem, our answer is hidden in plain sight.

The feelings of incompleteness or aloofness from within is an indication that we need to seek answers to our personal questions, even if we think that we have it all together. If we have a desire to run with the Big Boys or Girls in corporate America, we cannot wear our feelings on our shoulder, and we must be able to think on our feet. If we are indecisive from within, it may cross contaminate our professional repertoire;

therefore, we must engage in a routine checkup from the neck up.

Always keep in mind, we are emotional beings, and we are driven by the hidden desire to understand. Understand what? Understand self, understand life, understand people, understand our job, and the list goes on. From time to time, we all become restless about something or someone; it is a part of life. So, don't become dismayed when the questions of life are upon us—it is natural. In my opinion, this is where the power of our growth process is strengthened because we are designed to grow, learn, and share during our discovery process of answering our own questions of life. If questions are not asked or answered, we will become stagnant in our ability to truly understand self, and we will begin to depend on others for their acceptance, approval, or opinion. For example, here are a few questions to ask:

1. Are you truly happy with your life? Why?
2. Do you love your job? Why?
3. Do you know the meaning of your life? If not, why?
4. Is your job financially rewarding? If not, why?
5. Are you at the pinnacle of your success? If not, why? And what can you do differently?
6. What are your obstacles in life? Why?
7. Do you have a social life? If not, why?
8. Do you have time for your hobbies? If not, why?
9. Are you truly fulfilled in your relationships? Why?
10. Are you living your dream? If not, why?

These are a few questions to get you to understand the process of the "Why" questions. Do the "Why" questions really work? The answer is yes. Once we understand the reasons why we are doing what we do, we are better able to find the solution.

The freedom and flexibility of having the confidence of understanding the hidden secrets of the heart, it creates a platform to rise above those who are clueless about where they are going or what they are doing. In the midst of my Corporate Hustle, here are a few things my "Why" has taught me:

1. I had to value working on self to become better
2. I had to get rid of my limiting beliefs.
3. I had to adjust my perception.
4. I had to get rid of the bad/negative energy.
5. I had to change the way I think.
6. I had to learn the art of connecting with all types of people.
7. I had to replace my bad habits with good ones.
8. I had to bring my life into a state of peace.
9. I had to embrace my inner joy.
10. I had to realize there is no lack in my life.
11. I had to overcome all of my hidden fears.
12. I had to overcome doubt with positive action or affirmations.
13. I had to embrace the true elements of confidence.
14. I used my obstacles or setbacks as learning opportunities.
15. I learned how to become grateful for everything in life, which includes the little things.

16. I learned the power of letting go of people, places, and things that are not meant for me.
17. I learned the power of embracing and creating a powerful inner circle.
18. I have learned how to take action when necessary and to back off when needed.
19. I have learned the power of not violating my conscience.
20. I have learned to create a win-win situation out of everything.

The "Why" questions challenge our belief system, as well as our ability to own our truth. If we take a look at our habits, we will find that our habits are linked to our senses of seeing, hearing, touching, tasting, or smell in some way. For example:

1. Why can't Joe stop calling Sally? In all actuality, Sally is saying what Joe likes hearing. She is subconsciously filling an emotional need for Joe, and the moment he tries to pull away, the desire for the sound of her voice is like music to his ears. So, no matter what Sally does, he will keep calling her.
2. Why can't Bill stop wasting time looking at expensive sports cars he can't afford? Bill happens to like looking at expensive cars, hoping one day he would hit the lottery to buy one.
3. Why can't Ramona stay away from her side piece? She longs to be touched by her husband, but he thinks she has gained too much weight; and, he does not have a desire to touch her. Therefore, her extramarital affair with her side piece gives her the pleasures that she does not receive at home.

4. Why can't Jackie stop eating junk food? Jackie has a fear of being hungry. She developed her fear of going hungry when she was a child, after going several days without having anything to eat. To my amazement, she keeps a backlog of snacks hidden to ensure that she would not have to face the sting of hunger again. Like clockwork, every two hours, her taste buds will send her a signal when it is craving unhealthy junk food. This is a habit the no one can get Jackie to break because she has associated this habit with pain.
5. Why can't Jose stop buying fried chicken when he goes grocery shopping? When Jose walks into the grocery store, the smell of fried chicken seeping through the air vents makes him hungry. Even after many complaints from his wife, he chooses not to resist the temptation of buying it, because chicken is his comfort food.

There is a symbolic reason behind every action here that is triggered by our senses. If we take the time to question things, we will find that we are in control of more than we think.

CHAPTER 14

THE POWER OF MANAGING EXPECTATIONS

Superficial expectations leave room for disappointment or resentment when we feel as if we are under-appreciated, overlooked, rejected, or forgotten. If we become grateful for everything with an understanding that no one owes us anything, but we owe it to the world to give and do our best. Trust me, our mindset will shift, it will change our narrative, and we will not experience the element of disappointment.

In my opinion, in today's world, I have found people with less are happier than the people who have more. Why is this the case? The ones who have less do not have expectations of more. They understand they do not have it, so they do not worry about it while choosing to live a good life instead, as well as being grateful for what they have or what they get. Then the ones with more are always expecting more and more, to the point where greed is consuming them. Sadly, they are willing to do anything to get what they want by any means necessary.

Throughout my corporate journey, there is a serious battle with keeping our ego in check. It is so easy to get caught up in the elements of vanity, bragging about where we have been, what we are doing, where we are going, what we have, what we are getting, and so on. Never realizing that we are so caught up in TRYING to appear better while forgetting to express our sense of gratefulness. Although things are indeed nice to have, but showboating can come off as being a little arrogant, and it can turn some people off.

What I have found is that humility works a whole lot better than arrogance. The "What can I do to help you?" attitude makes our journey even better. This does not make us appear weak; actually, it exudes confidence instead. However, we definitely need to find balance in this area as well, because the lack of confidence can cause us to miss out on great opportunities. In my opinion, we never want to allow our lack of confidence to hinder our ability to move on to uncharted territory, or for us to become a liability as opposed to an asset.

Can we build our lives around our confidence? The answer is yes...if it is well-governed by our humbleness of thoughts, actions, and reactions. If we do not hold ourselves to a higher regard, then who will? Exactly! No one; and if they do, it is conditional. We must take care of ourselves mentally, physically, emotionally, and spiritually. If we are imbalanced in one of these four areas, we will have to overcompensate in one of the other areas, which can cause some form of instability.

Plus, we can become easily distracted or discouraged in that particular area as well. What are the signs of being imbalanced?

1. Depression.
2. Anxiety.
3. Not eating or overeating.
4. Feeling hopeless.
5. Discouraged.
6. Constantly negative.
7. Reclusiveness.
8. Abusiveness.
9. Self-harm.
10. Sudden skin or digestive disorders.

We are all going to feel these emotions from time-to-time. Nevertheless, it is our responsibility to recognize the signals of becoming imbalance to ensure we are able to narrow down the "Why" factor immediately. This will indeed cut back on the time it would take to bounce back; and, we are better able to get back to our happy state of being a whole lot quicker.

The epitome of real confidence comes from within; and when we are confident, we learn to respect the differences in others. We don't have to like their differences, but we must respect them. We never know what God is using to push them to the next level in life. Our way may not be God's way; therefore, we need to learn how to ask thought-provoking questions that give them something to think about or give them a bit of homework to do. In my opinion, this is a respectful way of building their level of confidence without them feeling as if we are better than them, degrading them, or being negative. The best gift our confidence can ever give to anyone is the opportunity to develop from the inside out.

When we are able to inject confidence, along with humbleness of positive energy into our projects, plans, systems, and strategies, we will find it creates a synergy that's beyond what we could ever imagine. There are so many ways to create a wow-factor in all we do; but more importantly, we cannot leave out the "What" and the "Why" factor.

From my experience, most of my "NO" projects came from a lack of understanding. So, in my revision process, I focused on answering their questions before they are asked, and I painted a crystal-clear picture of what I was conveying while ASSUMING the close. As a result, my "YES" projects have superseded the "NO" projects in my personal and professional life.

It took a lot of practice to master this process, but I was committed to *"The Corporate Hustle."* I always kept pen and paper with me to capture the thoughts, notes, and inspirations that were derived from all of my "NO" projects, to proactively overcome any objections beforehand. Does proactiveness work? Absolutely, we must take the time to do our homework to build our level of confidence to know and understand that we are in this hustle to win. It is imperative that we grow and develop to become stronger, wiser, resourceful, and useful in the areas of our giftings, talents, skills, or expertise.

CHAPTER 15

THE LEGACY OF PRESTIGE

Throughout *"The Corporate Hustle,"* we definitely do not want our legacy to end with us. We need to leave a trail of wisdom for the next generation. It does not matter how significant or insignificant we think our legacy is, we all have something to pass on to build the lives of others, personally or professionally. In my opinion, we are all icons in our own right, and our achievements mean something. There are a lot of people that would give anything to be where we are today; therefore, it is our reasonable service to provide the tools needed for them to build a legacy of their own.

Our daily lives are significant; we cannot discount the fact we are so blessed. Even though, we may have our ups and downs in life; but for the most part, we have a lot of reasons to be grateful. Now my question is, "What would you like for people to remember about you?" Yes, you! Hopefully, it is not materialistic, but the question needs an answer from YOU. If for some reason, people remember more of the negative character traits than the positive, then you have time to turn it around in your favor. Keep in mind, it is good and bad in everyone, but your good must outweigh the bad, period!

When we operate in love, kindness, compassion, and fairness, we gain a few notches under our belt, even if no one is saying anything—the human heart knows the truth! It is often said, "People will forget what we did, but they will not forget how we made them feel." When we are able to walk in another person's shoes when passing judgment or making decisions, we will learn how to approach the situation effectively. The soft approach does work when we learn how to speak the language of the person we are speaking with—this includes when we have to fire, dismiss, or break up with someone as well.

In my opinion, every time we come in contact with a person, we leave an impression upon their heart. If our stamp is not a good one, the time is now to make the adjustments necessary to encourage others through our words, actions, and behaviors. Most often, we think we have to do something massive, but in all reality, it is the little small things we do on a daily basis that makes the most profound impact. However, keep in mind, this is either positive or negative! Nevertheless, for the purpose of *"The Corporate Hustle,"* we are going to stay on the positive side of the spectrum, right?

Our legacy is not all about what people think of us; it is about what we think and feel about ourselves that influence the people around us. If for some reason our flaws are leaning toward the negative side of the spectrum, we need to focus on adjusting our character traits, shifting them from negative to positive. For example:

- If we are hateful, be nice.
- If we are rude, be kind.
- If we ignore others, then pay attention.
- If we are disruptive, then remain calm.
- If we are bad, then be good.
- If we are unkind, be kind.
- If we feel unloved, then love.

The list goes on...nevertheless, whatever we are dealing with, focus on the positive side of it. Learning the opposite of words or character traits will help us tremendously. If the investment into a book of antonyms would help, then by all means, do so. This has enabled me to reverse the role of a situation or the perception of my situation by 100%, as well as revamping my thoughts and self-talk.

We can pretend all we like; it is indeed the negative thoughts and self-talk that gets us in trouble personally and professionally. Keep in mind, our actions or reactions are based upon our thoughts, as well as our private self-talk. Therefore, when it comes down to corporate America or our legacy, we must govern it accordingly to ensure that any form of negativity does not make it into reality, making self-control of the utmost importance.

I have often heard the colloquialism, "Loose lips, sink ships." When we pride ourselves on degrading, criticizing, shaming, bullying, or laughing at others to boost our ego, it is a possibility we could be grafting this sort of behavior into our legacy. Now, if this is what is desired, then that is fine; however, for the sake of *"The Corporate Hustle,"* these negative character traits must be put on the backburner. In order to maximize our full potential, we must be willing to lend a helping hand, encourage, inspire, and mentor others who are in need of what we have to offer. We do not have to be perfect; we only need to be WILLING.

In my opinion, the most powerful legacy to leave behind is one of great substance. When we leave behind good character traits, wisdom, love, peace, kindness, compassion, mercy, goal setting, and self-control with a Positive Mental Attitude, there is no limit on what a person can achieve. This is a viable way to equip our future to keep on giving back after its own kind. I know it takes money to make the world go around; however, without substance, it will make us miserable.

Always remember, money is currency or provision; it is not substance, and it is not a vision. We must equip our legacy holders with the tools needed to maximize their substance or vision from the inside out. Listen, leaving behind the quality of life is by far the best gift we could ever give to anyone. When we are able to extract the hidden wisdom from within, as well as from life, greatness is inevitable regardless of who we are, where we are from, or our past mistakes.

Our life skills, work skills, creative skills, or people skills are all viable ways to impart the Law of Reciprocity. When we are able to share with others, the flood gates of wisdom will begin to share more of what we are giving. For example, if we have a desire to become better at something, if we share our becoming better with others who are trying to do the same, we will become better based upon the Biblical Principle of seed, time, and harvest. This is what worked for me in corporate America, and it will definitely work for those who capitalize on this principle.

How do we know if our legacy is missing something? When we are out of purpose, when we are not living up to our full potential, or when we are not tapping into our creativity, there is a secret longing from within that most people do not discuss with anyone. But, our first question to ourselves will be, "Why am I here?" We can indeed have the ideal life, the perfect family, the forever home, the dream job, the most beautiful car on the road, and the best friends ever. Yet, there is something missing, and it is secretly haunting us where we cannot enjoy the blessings that are before our very eyes.

Being blinded by reality or the inner longing from within can become devastating or traumatizing for some because they don't know what to do or which direction to turn. To be honest, most of corporate America is feeling this same way, but we cannot talk about it because we have what appears to be the perfect and the most sought-after lifestyle. So, what do we do? We do what everyone else does; we go searching for meaning. Some go about it the right way and some the wrong way—it is indeed this search that has brought most to *"The Corporate Hustle."* It is a real hustle, and make no mistake about it, everything in life that has real meaning or value, we will have to work for.

When leaving a legacy, make sure your will is written, documented, and duly recorded with the appropriate beneficiaries. Document everything! And, if you have a desire to leave a legacy outside of your family circle, here are a few ways to do so:

1. Write a book.
2. Write a song.
3. Write poems.
4. Write quotes.
5. Share your creativity on social platforms, such as YouTube, Facebook, Instagram, etc. Just make sure it will outlast you.
6. Start your own support group.
7. Become a speaker.
8. Create workshops.
9. Start a company.
10. Start a mentoring program.
11. Set up scholarships for those in need.
12. Become a donor.

Keep in mind, if we are successful in spite of mistreating or abusing others—just imagine how much more successful we could become if we were kind. All success is not good, and all success is not bad. If we are falling on the negative side of the spectrum, the time is now to step up our game to the positive side. We never want to sabotage ourselves, our family, our company, our employees, or any aspect of our lives for the lack of respect and dignity.

CHAPTER 16

LIVING OUR BEST LIFE

We all have problems, and we will all have something to work on or work toward. So, there is no need for us to feel as if we are the only one going through challenges, even though it may feel that way. What I have found is that in order to live our best life, we must understand it is possible. If we do not have hope in our possibilities, we place ourselves in a position to ward off what's coming next as opposed to living a fulfilled life.

It is exhausting to have to live our lives on guard or paranoid about what life is going to throw at us; therefore, we build walls where nothing can get in, and nothing can get out. Is this really living, or is this just existing? As a part of "*The Corporate Hustle*," this form of mindset stops here!

There is no need to envy the lives of others because we never know what is going on behind closed doors. So, it behooves us to come into the mindset of living our best life. If other families are happy about life, so can we; and, there is no need to compare our happiness with the next person because we are all unique. Besides, it is the joy from within that makes the real difference in our happiness. Listen, anyone can pretend to be happy, but we cannot pretend to have joy.

Joy is the silent motivation from within exhibited in our character. For example, I had a friend who appeared to be elated with happiness; she had everything a woman could ever ask for. She often bragged about her family and would often say, "She could not have asked for a more perfect life." As time went on, during a conference, I ran into her. She was extremely excited to tell me about her upcoming projects; so, I invited her to a cup of coffee.

As we sat down at the table, in the middle of our conversation, her son called. She reluctantly answered, then asked her son, "What do you want?" Her tone of voice threw me off while her facial expressions threw me even further. It appeared as if all of the happiness she spoke about, got up, and walked away from the table as she talked to her child in such a demeaning manner.

I was in a state of shock...here I am in front of the woman whose happiness I envied, and I am now seeing her true colors unfold before my very eyes. At this moment, I knew her happiness was a façade, and her character became very real.

I thought to myself, "How could she treat and speak to non-family members better than she did her child?" After months of research, I found that she was living her dream life at work and going home to a living nightmare that was zapping all of her joy. She did not know how to balance her personal and professional life. As a result, she put all of her energy into her professional life while blocking out her own.

I tried to assist in helping to bring balance to her life, but she insisted her life was just fine, and she did not need my help. Her children and her husband were treating her the exact same way she was treating them—it was their normal. With or without my help, this woman has changed the trajectory of my life, causing me to seek joy and peace from within while balancing my personal and professional life. As a life lesson for myself, I am now able to share this story with those who are in *"The Corporate Hustle"* like we are.

Believe it or not, we have so much control over our lives that we simply do not maximize. We opt for the norm; yet, we are able to opt for the phenomenal as well. How do we obtain a phenomenal life? In my opinion, if we find our element of creativity or gifting, it will change how we view life, and it will give our lives the true meaning of greatness.

We do not have to be a millionaire; we do not have to overextend ourselves with debt, we do not have to be smart, etc.; we simply need to be willing to find a way to finance our creativity. Just keep in mind, our creativity may or may not include our hobbies. How do we know the difference? Hobbies usually bring us peace or a moment for self. Whereas, our creativity usually challenges our mind to create something unique or bring forth a passion for helping or benefiting the lives of others. Here is a chart to help you better narrow down your passion.

The
CORPORATE
HUSTLE

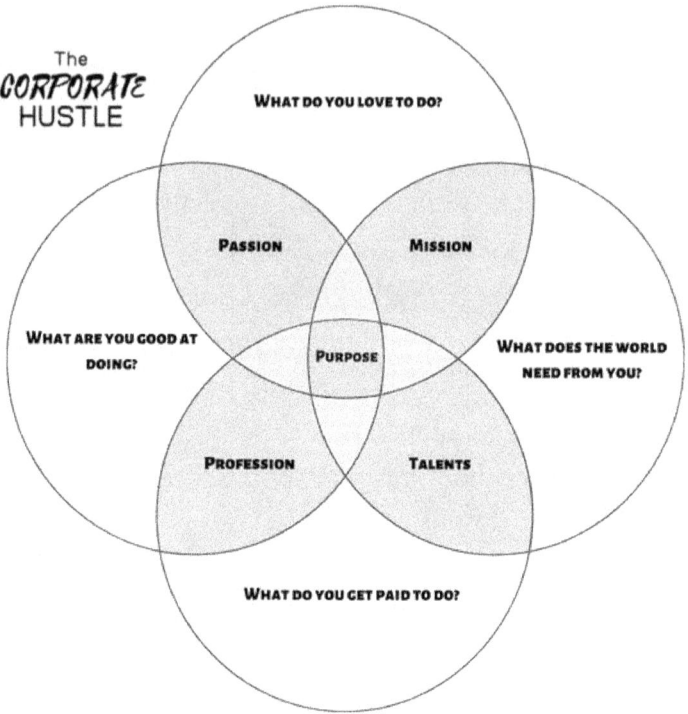

WHAT DO YOU LOVE TO DO?

PASSION

MISSION

WHAT ARE YOU GOOD AT DOING?

PURPOSE

WHAT DOES THE WORLD NEED FROM YOU?

PROFESSION

TALENTS

WHAT DO YOU GET PAID TO DO?

You are not limited to just these questions; you will still need to do the "what, when, where, how, and why" questions. There are times when you may need to add in the "Who" question as well.

CHAPTER 17

THE CORPORATE CINEMA

Our objective is not to crumble when we are rejected, criticized, embarrassed, insulted, or thrown under the bus. As a part of *"The Corporate Hustle,"* we may bend, but we do not break! Always remember, oxygen to the brain, will help us to stay calm if we find ourselves in a sticky situation. Really? Yes, really! Deep breathing helps, smiling, laughing, and then exercising. We cannot fall to pieces over people, places, and things when we do not get what we want...we cannot explode or implode based upon the thoughts and opinions of others.

The corporate cinema is always open and ready for the next hot topic. It is imperative that we control our negative emotions of anger, rage, hatred, etc. to ensure we are able to think on our feet while gaining control over our thoughts. This form of mental and emotional management will assist us in thinking through, as well as thinking beyond the situation, circumstance, or events that are placed before us.

Our internal movie screen is always ready and on cue to playback a mental image of what is taking place between our two ears. For this reason, we must always become cognizant of our thoughts and emotions. Furthermore, if our thoughts or emotions make it into reality with our actions, reactions, or attitude, we give everyone a bird's eye view of what is playing on our internal movie screen.

Often enough, I find those who say, "I can't control myself," yet, they have enough self-control to get up and go to work. They have enough self-control to pay their mortgage and car payments. They have enough self-control to pick and choose who they are in a relationship with. So, I came to a conclusion, they do have self-control in some areas and choosing not to use it in the areas that deal with their internal cinema. Here are a few things we can control:

1. We are in control of our thoughts.
2. We are in control of our actions.
3. We are in control of our reactions.
4. We are in control of our creativity.
5. We are in control of the paths we take in life.
6. We are in control of our happiness and joy.
7. We are in control of the lessons we learn or choose not to learn.
8. We are in control over converting our failures into win-win situations.
9. We are in control of the decisions we are making.
10. We are in control of the instructions we give ourselves.

11. We are in control of our change.
12. We are in control of our empowerment.
13. We are in control of our source of contribution back into society.
14. We are in control over mapping out our legacy.

We are in control of more things than we give ourselves credit...for example if we say cake, we associated with a birthday. When we say Hawaii, we associate it with a vacation. When we say oops, we associated with "What happened?" These are all related to our internal programming.

As a child, I wondered for years the reason why I craved popcorn at the movie theater and not at home. To my amazement, the smell of popcorn stimulated my desire to have it. Did I have control over it? Yes, but I did not realize it at the time; therefore, I gave in to it. According to my way of thinking at the time, it seemed as if popcorn and movies went together, but when I watch television, this association was never an option. Here are a few things that stimulate us:

1. Words
2. Pictures
3. Tones
4. Sounds
5. Smells
6. Tastes

The internal programming from our past, our environment, our beliefs, our experiences, our fantasies, our dreams, our hopes, our aspirations, and the list goes on—they are all contributing factors in who we are today. Now, get this, we take all of this into corporate America…and all of the unresolved issues are lingering in the workplace. So, my question is, "How can we make an impact without stirring up negative traumas, pains, or biases?" This is indeed a tough one…nevertheless, it is always best to stay in our lane, stay away from the gossip, live our best life, and stick to the positive side of the spectrum. We cannot fix them; we can only fix ourselves and share the positive experiences of love, compassion, and mercy.

The goal is to leave everyone better off than when we met them. We can inspire others by respecting their space. Barging into the lives of others to gossip about them or throw them under the bus is a big no-no! Karma is real…if we do not want someone to do that to us, then do not open the door to this sort of behavior. If we do engage in this by fault or default, in a matter of time, the corporate cinema will play it back, guaranteed!

Our corporate image is extremely important; it is not about what they are saying about us, it is about what we are saying, doing, and becoming while on or off the clock.

CHAPTER 18

THE POWER OF MIND MAPPING

We all want the perfect job or to open the ideal business to feel accomplished. But one thing I have found on this journey is that we must plan for it. I created a mind map of what I wanted; then I got it mapped out on paper, like a treasure map. It is through the very mind map that brought me to the treasure point of writing this book. If I can do it, so can you…I will show you how.

What is mental mapping or mind mapping? It is the process of mapping out your thoughts on paper like a business plan, but it is a little easier to glance at. Here's what you do:

1. Decide on the goal, then place it in the goal box.
2. Then answer the what, when, where, how, and why's of the goal.

For now, I would suggest you do a separate map for each goal; but keep them in the same Mind Map Binder.

We all have spent an insurmountable amount of time pondering over our next move, our next step, our next strategy, or next whatever. In this process, what I have found is that we all have a desire to change something in some way. Wishes are good, dreams are divine, but an action plan gives us leverage or positioning to move forward. This is where goals come into play; and, we all know what goals are, as well as the reason for them. However, most often, our follow-through is the deterrent from accomplishing the goal.

I have found that we do set goals daily without realizing they are goals, which get accomplished like clockwork. For example, waking up in the morning—our goal is to get up at a specific time, take care of our morning duties, get dressed, and go to work. Goal accomplished, right? Okay, let's take a look at when we leave work, is it not a goal to leave at a particular time? Once we leave, goal accomplished, right? I call it the subliminal goals because we are not aware of what we are doing, so we get it done, especially when it is connected to our livelihood. But the moment we say goal, our mind may put up a subconscious block to avoid accomplishing our goals.

It is amazing how our mind will create mental blocks when we associate certain words with our actions. For this reason, it is best to learn how to mind map. It provides a mental guide to navigate through every aspect of our lives, including:

- Family.

- Health/Fitness.
- Wealth/Finances.
- Work/Career.
- Success.
- Relationships.
- Self-esteem.
- Self-control.

The list goes on...there is no limit on what we can achieve once we plan to do so. Trust me, once we can map out our journey, we will experience:

- Less stress.
- Less anxiety.
- Less dead ends.
- Fewer disappointments.
- Less anger/frustration.
- More accomplishments.
- More structure.
- More confidence.
- More happiness.
- Better discipline.
- Better concentration/focus.
- Better performance.
- Better results.
- Better satisfaction.

If we learn how to mind map by priority, we are able to get things done quicker. In order to maximize this process, I suggest selecting the most important, the quickest, and the most relevant. Why do we put the quickest before the most relevant? There are times when we can accomplish certain things by multi-tasking. These are usually the things we can squeeze in when we are waiting on something or someone as opposed to wasting time.

Regardless of whether we are doing corporate, personal, prospect, or restructural mapping or planning; it is easier, memorable, and effective. Bottom line, mind mapping creates a step-by-step guide at a glance.

This process works for everyone; it is not limited to the corporate workplace, high achievers, business people, the elite, etc. All we need is a vision, motivation, Positive Mental Attitude, and a willingness to execute. Here is what I used to mind map my interviews:

At the end of the day, plan your tasks for the following day. This allows you to get a running start for the next morning without wasting hours trying to decide where to start or which way to turn. Also, it gives you a dedicated amount of time to strategize, review goals, and allow problem-solving opportunities. It works for me, and it can definitely work for you. Try spending about forty-five minutes at the end of your business day in the office to plan your tasks for the following day. You will notice about 95% of the employees have left for the day; it gives you a little quiet time. Also, this allows you to debrief activities from that day, and your reputation as a hard worker stays intact. Not to mention the end of day traffic may have decreased, yielding the possibility of a more at ease drive home.

With or without goals written down, we subconsciously make them without realizing it; however, the key is to find what makes us tick. Meanwhile, the ticktock of our daily goals continue with or without our permission; we need to take control to navigate accordingly. If not, life will dictate our path as opposed to being able to set our own stage.

As a congruent part of "The Corporate Hustle," we must get into the mindset of aligning our future goals as well. We do not want to complete our daily to-do lists without taking our other goals into consideration. In the preparation or self-improvement phase, we must develop our mind-eye coordination, which requires us to step outside our comfort zone. Mind-eye coordination is being able to get what we see in our mind to line up with what we see with our physical eyes.

In short, we need to get our perception and our vision to communicably line up with each other.

The ability to positively communicate with our vision is muchly sought after by those who understand the power of having a Positive Mental Attitude. As a word from the chronicles of corporate wisdom, the best way to improve our communication skills is to master the communication with self. Once we fully understand the intricacies of our mind, we are better able to articulate the desires of our heart, as well as become a desirable commodity to share what we know. When mind mapping using S.M.A.R.T. Goals, here is what we need:

- We need to know the what, when, where, how, and why's of our goals.
- We need to be able to listen effectively. Even if it sounds a little crazy, don't worry—write it down, and sort it out later.
- We need to become humble.
- We need to understand that we are all subjected to err on occasion. So, if a mistake is made, we need to understand it, laugh about it, or joke about it, and keep moving!
- We need to overcome our excuses.
- We need to make direct eye contact when speaking to others, or when talking to self in the mirror.
- We need to add a little humor into our lives.
- We need to interact with others with a note pad in hand. We never know when or how the elements of wisdom will flow to us; so, we must be prepared.

- We need to learn how to smile in order to release our creative juices, as well as our power of expression. This may sound a little corny, but it works!
- We need to set an example for others, as well as share our process of setting goals.
- We need to prepare the way for our success. Our success logbook should be riddled with notes, ideas, concepts, precepts, etc. If this is not the case, get busy.

You are indeed on the leading edge of whatever your mind can conceive…you cannot fall when your creative giant from within is in full armor or when it has your back! Regardless of where you are in life, your goals need to be **S**pecific, **M**easurable, **A**ttainable, **R**elevant, and **T**imely. Here is an example:

The
CORPORATE
HUSTLE

WORKING TOWARDS S.M.A.R.T. GOALS

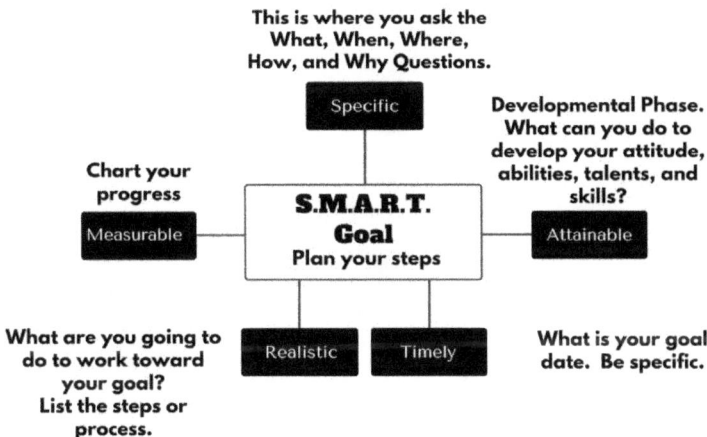

This is where you ask the What, When, Where, How, and Why Questions.

Specific

Developmental Phase. What can you do to develop your attitude, abilities, talents, and skills?

Chart your progress

Measurable

S.M.A.R.T. Goal
Plan your steps

Attainable

What are you going to do to work toward your goal? List the steps or process.

Realistic   Timely

What is your goal date. Be specific.

CHAPTER 19

PROCRASTINATION

In *"The Corporate Hustle,"* if we find ourselves procrastinating, we must ask ourselves fact-finding questions to overcome the inner block, distraction, or habit. To be honest, some of our procrastination can be a result of our laziness. I am so guilty of this from time-to-time, but I have mastered ways to push myself beyond by self-imposed limitations. Here are a few ways that I have found to maximize my effectiveness and productivity:

1. I own it. The moment we are in denial of our procrastination…it gives room to excuses.
2. I get rid of stress or anxiety. If we cannot get rid of stressful people, places, and things, seek inner peace.
3. I eliminate any form of guilt or resentment associated with the element of procrastination.

4. I narrow down the reasons for procrastinating. This would be the "Why" questions.
5. I develop a mind map to redirect the strategy or system of achievement.

What are the common indications that we are procrastinating?

1. When we are always making excuses.
2. When we are indecisive.
3. When we are critical of others, and we are not contributing.
4. When we are a perfectionist; if the situation is not perfect, we don't do anything.
5. When we stress out or have panic attacks.
6. When we self-sabotage projects or goals.
7. When we do not listen, learn, or apply.
8. When we fear the element of failure.
9. When we are unorganized.
10. When we are a bully.
11. When our worth is based on the right materialistic condition.
12. When we are feeling hopeless.

Procrastination is really our negative self-talk overworking our mind, causing it to shut down or block out people, places, and things that pertain to our goals.

Fear, laziness, doubt, and lack of motivation or interest contributes to us putting off things or negative self-talk. And, regardless of how we sugarcoat our procrastination, we will find it falls under at least one of these categories. One of the keys to our greatness is to be able to own our truth. This gives us the ammunition to counteract the desired outcome in our personal or professional life.

We all value our quality of life to a certain extent, but we are not all willing to put in the extra work needed to attain what we desire. In my opinion, by not going the extra mile or putting in the extra work, we will find ourselves overlooking or missing opportunities. This will sometimes add to our level of frustration causing us to give up or not try at all subconsciously. Even if that happens to us from time-to-time, we have the power to overcome it at any given moment by making a choice to do so. Is it that easy? The choice is indeed that easy; however, our accomplishments may take a little work. But if we create a to-do list of our daily tasks, it becomes easier. I promise!

CHAPTER 20

MAGNETIC APPEAL

Corporate America is driven by success and leadership. Being this is the case; it should not cause anyone to become dismayed. We are all successful at something, and we all have a leader from within. So, regardless of the perception of corporate elites, we are all here to assist each other in becoming and being our best.

I have always heard we are able to capture more bees with honey. Is this an accurate statement? Absolutely...we must possess a magnetic effect. How do we become magnetic? It begins with our mindset, our attitude, our character, and our ability to share. If we give people what they want, they will provide us with what we want. Keep in mind, we will have those who try to resist the effect; however, that is not our problem. Simply, move on to the natural flow of guided energy; we do not have time to convince or fight with people.

In order to keep our magnetism of effectiveness, we must be at peace from within.

Humility…humility…humility…is the honey! When I break down honey, it says to me HONE into the Y! If we can answer the "Why" of our magnet, it gives us the ability to believe it. If we want to have a magnetic personality just because…it is not going to cut it! Listen, this book is called *"The Corporate Hustle,"* and we make smart moves. Now, in order to do so, the "Just Because" is not an option…we must be "In The Know."

Experience and knowledge do account for something; however, we must be able to implement. From my experience, a down-to-earth strategy of execution is a pivotal way of differentiating the ordinary from the extraordinary.

We all have what it takes to become and remain successful if we are willing to learn, prepare, become disciplined, teach, and share. Throughout my "Corporate Hustle," here are a few things I want to share:

1. Discipline is a must.
2. Do not take rejection personally.
3. Get out of your feelings.
4. Use criticism as a learning tool.
5. Learn from your failure and create a win-win situation. There is always an element of wisdom left behind.
6. Become an excellent planner.
7. Set goals.
8. Take calculated risks.
9. Stay focused on what you are doing by limiting your distractions.
10. Learn the power of delegation.

The nature of our behavior plays a vital role in our level of success. If we think for a minute, we can ignore the consequences of our lack of dedication, think again. The sense of longing has a way of tugging at our inner core; so, it behooves us to hire a mentor or coach to assist in this area or once again, delegate.

Our supreme power of innovation is what keeps our creativity flowing. It does not matter if we are in the corporate arena or not; the essence of our potentiality is bottled up inside of us. Sadly, it is our character flaws that keep it hidden. Of course, we all have flaws, but there are certain character traits that contaminate our hustle. With this in mind, in order to win in the game of life, we must play our cards close to our chest. When we adversely allow others to see the cards in our hand, it is a possibility that we can give birth to a bed of doubt in whatever we are doing, saying, or becoming.

CHAPTER 21

THE PLAYING ZONES

We cannot get away from the choices of life and the games people play. We can opt out on making choices, which leaves room for someone to make them for us. We can opt out of engaging in the games people play, which leaves room for us to play ourselves short or to outright get played. What do we do when the challenge of the game is before our very eyes asking, "Do we want to live a fulfilled life, or do we want to have an unfulfilled one?" Do we get tongue tied or do we answer? If we decide not to answer, then life will call the shots. However, in my opinion, we should take authority, leaving no room to play ourselves short.

The power play moves of leverage can indeed work for us, or it can work against us, depending upon the perceived intention of the move. It can be a strategic or manipulative move, but if we do not play our cards right, we can indeed get ourselves moved into the no play zone or blackballed. If we think for a minute that we cannot get blackballed in the corporate world, we are sadly mistaken. We simply do not speak about it much, but it happens more than we care to imagine. In short, it behooves us to polish up our character traits to ensure that we are able to play with the Big Boys and Girls in corporate America.

If we have a desire to master the playing zones of corporate America, it is best that we hire a coach or mentor to empower us with the key concepts of leadership and etiquette. If we think for a minute that we play by our own rules, we are headed for the blackball list! When we are not on our own playing field, we must learn how to play by the key rules of the corporate game. If you think this is not a game, get too many strikes and see what happens! You got it…you will be out the door so fast; it will make your head spin.

"The Corporate Hustle" is designed to help you make strategic power play moves that create a win-win situation for all involved. But you need to know what keeps the passion burning inside of you. In my opinion, this is what makes you unstoppable at winning the desires of your heart.

The moment I see a person jumping from one thing to the next, it is an indication they are not 100% sure about their passion. Even if we are involved in a lot of things that are making money, and we are not sure if we have pinpointed our passion; we could be spinning our wheels overcompensating with material gain, status, titles, or paygrades. Nevertheless, the only person can give an account or the true answer will be the one who is involved in everything; while running from pillar to post searching for meaning when it is already within. Don't worry; I know this is not you because you have the information that you need to win at what you love doing, right? Of course.

The goal is to do everything in the spirit of excellence. According to *"The Corporate Hustle,"* you should not rush through things or rush to get things done. Take your time, and get into the mode of excellence; which means you should not half-do projects or rig them up. Big dreams are not built on rushing; they are built on precision; therefore, you must perfect the art of thoroughness. Rushing causes us to miss out on valuable lessons and steps that could create a huge setback, tattered dreams, or shattered inspirations.

Failure that could have been avoided is an indication of not playing our cards right or slipping in the game of life. This often happens when we are wallowing in a bed of doubt, fear, and limitation. We must work smart and hard at the same time in order to progress toward our desired destination without allowing envy or covetousness to take up residence in our heart and mind.

The mere reflections of our thoughts, emotions, beliefs, experiences, and inspirations are predicated on our good or bad decisions. If we need to grow, we know it. If we are making bad decisions, we know it. If we are engaging in something positive or negative, we know it. Regardless of what we are doing, we know it…we are just in denial of our knowing. Keep in mind, with any form of denial, it blocks our highest and greatest potential, as well as our true mastery.

As a part of "The Corporate Hustle," whether we are in or out of the game, self-growth and self-development for the better are a must. This helps to avoid becoming a victim of harmful or negative habits designed to keep us sifted away from greatness.

CHAPTER 22

UNDERSTANDING THE PLAN

The biggest obstacle I have found is that most of us doing business are not equipped with a business plan. A business plan can be used as a roadmap; as a matter of fact, it is also used as a promise to the cause of the business. When we are able to connect to the business, we are able to believe in what we are doing wholeheartedly. Most people in the corporate world are doing what they are told, doing things out of routine, only giving what's required to get a paycheck, or outright faking it.

The stress or dread of preparing a business plan can be eliminated by paying someone to prepare it as opposed to staring at a blank piece of paper trying to do it on our own. A professional business plan writer can save us a lot of time, but we need to be able to convey our thoughts, desires, and goals clearly. When deciding to choose someone, make sure that writing samples, testimonials, and free unlimited revisions are included before the final draft. Don't forget to understand the logistics of the fees, whether it is by the hour, per word, per page, or a flat fee. If you decide to do it on your own, here is what you will need:

- Executive Summary.
- Company Description.
- Market Analysis.
- Breakdown of Your Products and Services.
- Revenue Model.
- Operating Model.
- Competitive Analysis.
- Description of Management and Organization.
- Marketing Plan.
- Sales Strategy.
- Request for Funding.
- Financial Projections.

We are here to solve problems, not create them. If we do not have the answers, then it is our responsibility to hire those that do. This is what business is about...this is why we have business owners, employees, and consumers. We are all getting some sort of need filled or an answer to some kind of problem. It does not matter how we sugarcoat it; our growth or decline is predicated on needs, problems, and solutions. For example, let's take my need...here is what I ask myself to get my wheels turning:

1. What is the cause of the need?
2. Who can determine the need?
3. How can I resolve the need?
4. Why is it needed?
5. Where is the need applicable?
6. When is it needed?

We may have graduated from high school and college, but we have not graduated from the classroom. In my opinion, we never will. There are so many life lessons to learn that we cannot close the door on the classroom. In the world of business or in our personal lives, we need to continually educate ourselves in our field of expertise, while taking a logical approach.

When we are not able to truly define the problem, then we cannot truly find the solution. Therefore, it is imperative that we polish up our problem-solving skills to ensure we are able to break the problem down in order to get the right answers. Here's what I do:

1. I grab a piece of paper to define the problem.
2. I give God thanks for the problem and thanks in advance for the solution to that specific problem.
3. I write out the cause and effect.
4. I determine if it is positive or negative. If negative, I decide how I can make it positive.
5. I determine the objective. I proactively project my anticipated positive outcome.

6. I determine the viable resources I may need to accomplish the desired outcome.
7. I do a mind map for my action plan.
8. I prepare a plan-b, just to spark the creative side to check if I missed something.
9. I get feedback from others if necessary.
10. I then execute.

There is a reason why children ask so many questions…they are formulating their own thoughts based upon the answers they are receiving from us. As an adult, we tend to know everything, so we stop asking ourselves questions. As a result, we lose our platform of how to ask the right questions to provoke the element of our thought process, because we are too busy trying to get into the mind of others. If we have not mastered the aspect of problem-solving at its best, then we do not have time to analyze what's going on in the life of someone else. In my opinion, the mind-games of today is causing us to play ourselves short when it comes down to playing to win!

As a part of *"The Corporate Hustle,"* there is no lack…you have everything you need. I need you to believe this beyond a shadow of a doubt; if not, you can inadvertently attract the spirit of lack. Your thoughts must become positive in nature…if a negative thought creeps up, cancel it and replace it with a positive affirmation.

Fear, desperation, and neediness are distractions that are designed to deprive you of your prosperity. Therefore, it is best to believe that you are a success magnet and be willing to take calculated risks. Here is what I recite periodically during the day:

- God has given me the power to get wealth.
- Prosperity and abundance in every area of my life are here and now.

You can reach the pinnacle of your career or profession!

CHAPTER 23

LEADING THE FIELD

The follow-the-leader and do no more than I am told mentality is not the ideal criteria for leading our field. True leaders are developed and trained to lead with humility with a continuation of practice, enthusiasm, and commitment.

In my opinion, leadership is not about being on a power trip. It is about mentoring the up and coming leaders to lead by example with a clear sense of purpose while building the trust and confidence of their subordinates. When we have good business ethics and communication skills, we are able to develop excellent relationships with others.

The willingness to apply the tools and lessons of life gives us the opportunity to improve and succeed on a level beyond what we could have ever imagined. For the record, self-improvement is a pivotal element of success, leadership, and winning. In addition, there is another crucial element we cannot leave out called self-acceptance. In order to lead our field, we must be able to accept ourselves for who we are while polishing up the weak areas and making the stronger areas exceptional.

The step-by-step process of self-improvement may not make us an overnight sensation. It does give us the stability needed to dig deep within ourselves to take ownership of our strengths and weaknesses. By doing so, it pulls out our hidden greatness with the confidence of knowing we are not pretending, and we are the real deal; therefore, we will not have to second-guess our level of success. When we know we have paid the price and put in the work for being who we are today; we will have a level of unmatched appreciation for the process.

If we are still consumed by what people think as opposed to what we believe about ourselves or how we present ourselves to people, we have not arrived at the level of leadership. We can pretend to be a leader, mentor, or inspiration, but if we are leaving people emotionally or mentally wounded by our pompous behavior, we have not arrived at the desired level of leadership status. When truly leading our field, we must leave a trail of victors, not victims. In the corporate world, numbers talk! If we have a desire to lead, we must be willing to become humble enough to create an atmosphere of victory.

The road of success leaves a trail of victorious living, successful planning, and powerhouse legacies. We cannot become blinded by our wants and needs to the point where we don't see the wants and needs of others. Our ability to lead in excellence is comprised of the choices and decisions we make on our journey; however, on this journey, we must be able to set, measure, progress, and achieve. The muscle of our creativity must be exercised continuously to keep a steady flow; therefore, we must view our business plan, goals, or strategies periodically. This will help unleash a steady stream of positive energy that will attract what we are in agreement with mentally.

"The Corporate Hustle" has given you the opportunity to approach your personal and professional life in such a manner that will create a win-win situation for all involved. The fantastic wisdom found within the pages of this book will place anchors of great possibilities within your reach. So, it behooves you to take advantage of this valuable information to release your profound and unique creative hustle. You are only one idea away from your next breakthrough or miracle; therefore, lead your field with precision leaving no stone unturned.

CHAPTER 24

THE CORPORATE SEAL

We are not here to win a popularity contest; we are here to succeed at living our best life and creating the same for others. When we are able to decode the secrets hidden within our life's journey, we are better able to translate the teachable moments to those who are following in our footsteps.

In and out of our corporate life, opportunities are created and destroyed based upon our perception. It is indeed our perceived results that bring about our happiness or discontentment. If we change our overall perception to incorporate the seal, "We are blessed to bless others," it puts a prosperity seal on what we do, say, and become.

This information may be new for some; however, most do not take into account that there is a corporate seal place on a company. Take a moment to think about it; almost every organization is involved in some charity. They partner with or donate money, products, and services to other charitable organizations in exchange for a tax write off, as well as the hidden blessings. However, it goes a little deeper…their giving is based upon the Law of Reciprocity where we give to receive. Their giving is a symbolic way of tithing from a business standpoint and not necessarily from a religious one. Nonetheless, it works, and we should not be limited in our ability to share as well. In my opinion, giving is a great way to put the corporate seal on our lives with no shame attached, while becoming highly favored.

When understanding our personal or professional journey, our plans, and our solutions, we should consider how we are going to give back or pay it forward to the cause of our revolutionization. Although, in some instances, we may win or lose; we still need to come to a commonplace of sharing with others in spite of our ups and downs in life.

In conclusion, as a part of *"The Corporate Hustle,"* you are being held to a higher ethical standard. After reading this book, you have indeed raised the bar on how you think and maneuver throughout life. From this point on, no excuses! You have what you need to succeed in every area of your life; use the tools you have and never stop learning. From me to you, get your hustle on!

9 781948 936316